W9-CMC-832

THE STALINIST EMPIRE

THE STALINIST EMPIRE

THE RISE AND FALL OF THE SOVIET UNION

TED GOTTFRIED

ILLUSTRATED BY MELANIE REIM

TWENTY-FIRST CENTURY BOOKS
BROOKFIELD, CONNECTICUT

Photographs courtesy of Brown Brothers: p. 19; Culver Pictures, Inc.: pp. 25, 32; Süddeutscher Verlag Bilderdienst: pp. 41, 48, 70, 79, 99; © Getty Images: pp. 54 (Hulton/Archive), 59 (Archive), 96 (Keystone); © Bettmann/Corbis: p. 89. Map by Joe LeMonnier.

Library of Congress Cataloging-in-Publication Data
Gottfried, Ted.
The Stalinist empire / Ted Gottfried ; illustration by Melanie Reim.
p. cm. — (The Rise and fall of the Soviet Union)
Includes bibliographical references and index.
Summary: Chronicles the years of Joseph Stalin's iron-fisted reign in the Soviet Union, from the time of Lenin's death to the dawn of World War II.
ISBN 0-7613-2558-1 (lib. bdg.)
1. Soviet Union—History—1925-1953—Juvenile literature. [1. Stalin, Joseph, 1879-1953. 2. Soviet Union—History—1925-1953.] I. Reim, Melanie K., ill. II. Title.
DK267 .G668 2002 947.084'2—dc21 2001052251

Published by Twenty-First Century Books
A Division of The Millbrook Press, Inc.
2 Old New Milford Road
Brookfield, Connecticut 06804
www.millbrookpress.com

Printed in Hong Kong
5 4 3 2 1

DEDICATION

For my daughter,
Julie Coakley,
who stole my heart,
and has it still
—TG

ACKNOWLEDGMENTS

I am grateful to personnel of the New York Central Research Library, the Mid-Manhattan Library, the Society Library in New York City, and the Queensboro Public Library for aid in gathering material for this book. Thanks also to Dan Gottfried and Rudy Kornmann for bailing me out with their computer expertise and online research tips. Also, gratitude and much love to my wife, Harriet Gottfried, who—as always—read and critiqued this book. Her help was invaluable, but any shortcomings in the work are mine alone.

Ted Gottfried

CONTENTS

THE STALINIST EMPIRE

ARCTIC
Svalbard
GREAT BRITAIN
NORTH SEA
NORWAY
Franz Josef L
BELGIUM
NETHERLANDS
DENMARK
SWEDEN
Novaya Zemlya
GERMANY
Murmansk
BARENTS SEA
FINLAND
BALTIC SEA
KARA SEA
ESTONIA
LATVIA
LITHUANIA
Archangel
Leningrad
L. Onega
N. Dvina R.
URAL MTNS.
POLAND
Novy Port
Minsk
Smolensk
Moscow
Dnieper R.
Ob R.
Berezov
Kiev
ROMANIA
Volga R.
Oka R.
Kazan
Ob R.
Odessa
Dnepropetrovsk
Don R.
BULGARIA
Ekaterinburg
Crimea
Volga R.
Samara
UNION OF SOV
Sebastopol
Rostov
Tsaritsyn (Stalingrad)
Orenburg
BLACK SEA
Omsk
CAUCASUS MTS.
TURKEY
Astrakhan
Batum
Ekibastuz
CASPIAN SEA
Karaganda
ARAL SEA
Kazalinsk
SYRIA
Baku
Perovsk
Krasnovodsk
Tashkent
Ashkhabad
IRAQ
Andizhan
TRANSJORDAN
Merv
Samarkand
KUWAIT
PERSIA
ARABIA
Kushka
AFGHANISTAN

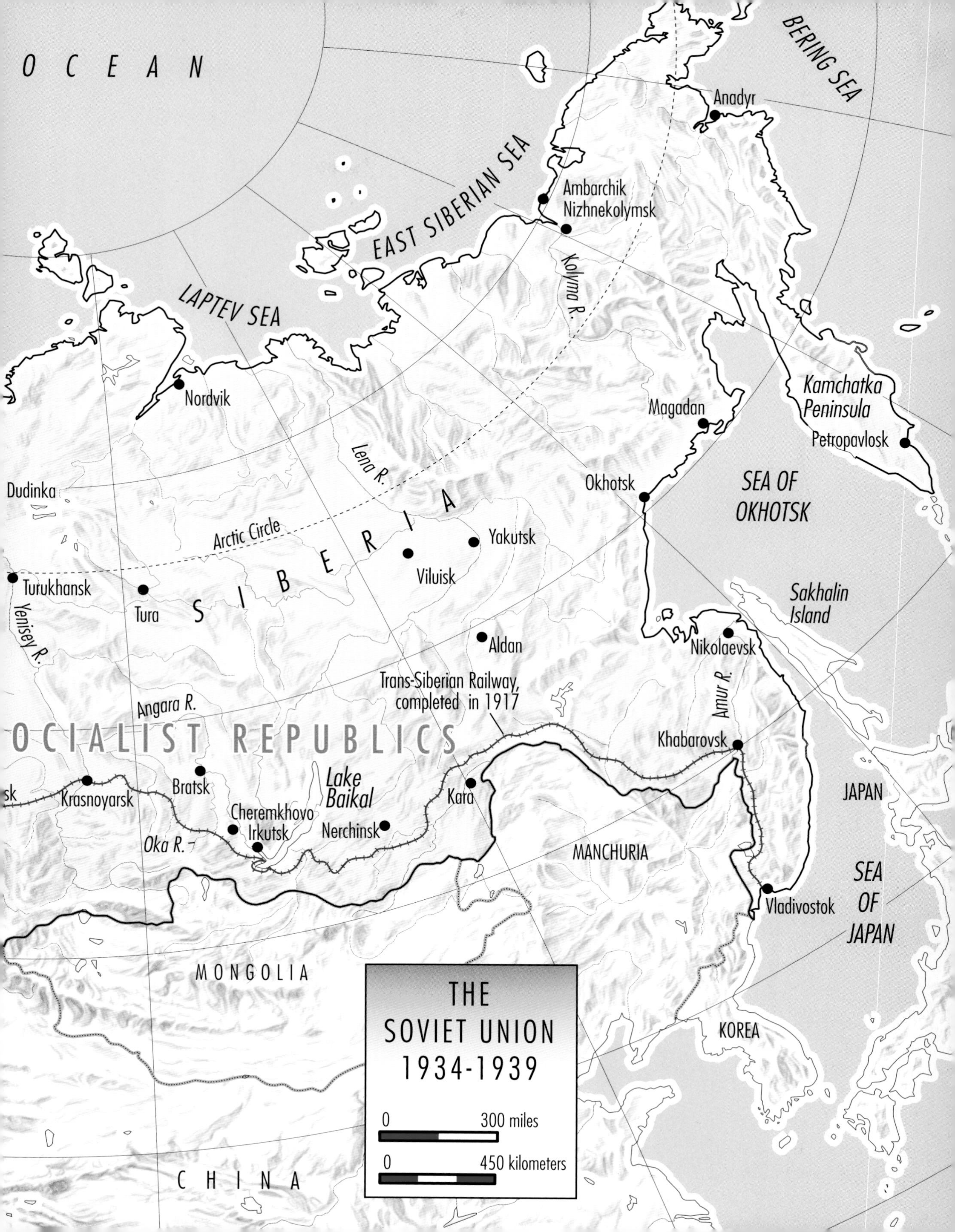
OCEAN
BERING SEA
EAST SIBERIAN SEA
LAPTEV SEA
Anadyr
Ambarchik
Nizhnekolymsk
Kolyma R.
Nordvik
Kamchatka Peninsula
Magadan
Petropavlosk
Lena R.
Okhotsk
SEA OF OKHOTSK
Dudinka
Arctic Circle
SIBERIA
Yakutsk
Viluisk
Turukhansk
Tura
Yenisey R.
Sakhalin Island
Aldan
Nikolaevsk
Trans-Siberian Railway, completed in 1917
Angara R.
Amur R.
OCIALIST REPUBLICS
Khabarovsk
Bratsk
Lake Baikal
Kara
JAPAN
sk
Krasnoyarsk
Cheremkhovo
Irkutsk
Nerchinsk
Oka R.
MANCHURIA
SEA OF JAPAN
Vladivostok
MONGOLIA
THE SOVIET UNION 1934-1939
KOREA
0
300 miles
0
450 kilometers
CHINA

PREFACE

The chronicle of Soviet Russia in the twentieth century shows how the destinies of a person and a nation can merge to affect the course of history. At its extreme, such a link is known as a "cult of personality." It is the complete identification of a nation with its leader. What is good for the leader is good for the nation. What is good for the nation is what the leader says is good for the nation. The good citizen follows the rules laid down by the leader. Refusal to conform is treason. Patriotism is defined as absolute loyalty to the leader.

For almost thirty years, the leader of the Soviet Union was Joseph Stalin. The nation he ruled was a poor land, which had overthrown tsarist tyranny to embrace a Socialist dream of adequate food, clothing, and shelter in a society built on equality and dignity. Under Stalin, the dream became a nightmare. Yet the people remained loyal through the Stalinist dictatorship, which brought them famine, persecution, purges, and death.

Millions died under Stalin's manipulation of the government and the people. Yet the identification of the nation with him remained firm. How did Stalin manage this? How did he maintain the cult of personality, which validated his power? Who was this man who claimed the soul of a nation only to consign it to oblivion? Who was Joseph Stalin?

CHAPTER ONE

SEIZING THE REINS

I was repelled by the very qualities which would strengthen him . . . the narrowness of his interests, his psychological coarseness, and the special cynicism of the provincial. . . .

Leon Trotsky's reaction
to Joseph Stalin

Early in the year 1924, Joseph Stalin sent a cable to his most powerful rival for control of the Russian Communist party: "Tell Comrade Trotsky that Comrade Lenin died suddenly on 21 January at six hours fifty. Death caused by paralysis of respiratory centre. Funeral 26 January. Stalin."[1]

Leon Trotsky did not attend the services. He later claimed that he had been tricked and given "the wrong date for the funeral." A French newspaper correspondent who was there believed that Trotsky had missed an important opportunity to outshine Stalin. "If Trotsky had come to Moscow," he wrote, "he would have stolen the whole show."[2]

ENSHRINING A COMMUNIST

It was quite a show even without Trotsky. For most Russians, Vladimir Ilich Lenin had embodied the success of the Russian Revolution. Since the Bolsheviks, as the Communists were originally known, had seized power in November 1917, he had been in command of the government through a bloody civil war followed by war with Poland, a typhus epidemic, and a famine, which had devastated the nation. Lenin was a tyrant, and he may not have been loved by the Russian people, but he was a symbol of their survival as a nation. His funeral was described by writer Nadezhda Mandelstam as "the Moscow of ancient days burying one of her tsars."[3]

The spectacle was conceived by Stalin. In his will Lenin had asked to be buried beside his mother. His wife, Krupskaia, "wanted no monument, no celebrations . . . no mausoleum." But Stalin, born a peasant, knew the Russian people better than Lenin, his wife, or any of the other top leaders of the Communist party. Under Lenin's direction, he had been one of those who supervised the brutal crackdown on organized religion—particularly the Russian Orthodox Church, to which most people in Russia belonged. Nevertheless, Stalin understood the need for faith, and for its trappings. The holy relics had been seized by the Communist government, but their absence left a vacuum. He recognized the need to cater to the peasants' belief "rooted in Orthodox religion, that the remains of saints were immune to decay."[4]

Following Lenin's death, his body lay in state in the Hall of Columns in Moscow. Tens of thousands of Russians slowly filed past it while plans went ahead for a service and burial. On January 26, Moscow's Bolshoi Theater was draped in black for a mourning ceremony. The packed hall heard Stalin declaim that "in leaving us, Comrade Lenin ordained us to guard the unity of our party like the apple of our eye. We vow to thee, Comrade Lenin, that we shall honorably fulfill this thy commandment." He spoke like a high priest, merging the language and cadence of discarded religion with the ideology of the Communist party.

The next day the population of Moscow poured into the streets to observe Stalin and other Communist leaders carry Lenin's coffin to the Kremlin wall. Here it was lowered into the vault, which was to be its temporary resting place. Eventually, it was to rest in Red Square, in a specially erected mausoleum with glass panels so that the leader's body might be viewed. However, before that could happen, the body began to decompose. Scientists worked frantically for three months to stabilize it with various combinations of embalming fluids. Meanwhile, Lenin's brain was transferred to the V. I. Lenin Institute, where it was dissected to discover the secrets of his "genius," and to prove that it was an example of "a higher stage in the evolution of mankind." His heart went to the V. I. Lenin Museum.[5]

Over the next couple of decades, many Russians came to Lenin's tomb to view the body. Some of them surreptitiously genuflected. Religion was persecuted in Russia, but it wasn't dead. Nevertheless, the crypt provided the first Communist example of the cult of personality. Joseph Stalin was to be its heir.

CONTAINING TROTSKY

Nobody could have predicted two years before Lenin's death that Stalin would replace him as master of the Union of Soviet Socialist Republics (USSR). At that time, after Lenin, the most powerful man in the Communist party was Leon Trotsky. He was brilliant; he was a war hero; his name was known to the people. Stalin was not a first-rate intellectual; he had disobeyed orders during the war with Poland and been reprimanded by Lenin for doing so; he was not as imposing a figure as Trotsky. Nevertheless, Lenin appointed Stalin general secretary of the party in April 1922.

By this time the twenty-one-member Central Committee of the Communist party had created a five-member Politburo to deal with matters too urgent to await discussion by the larger body. Three of the five were Lenin, Trotsky, and Stalin. The Politburo was soon making decisions in every area of government, bypassing the Central Committee and the workers' councils known as soviets. Using the excuse that quick action was imperative, the Politburo rode roughshod over all democratic and other opposition.

In May 1922, Lenin suffered the first of a series of strokes. A three-man leadership troika, which included Stalin, Grigori Zinoviev, and Lev Kamenev, headed the government in Lenin's absence. When Lenin recovered briefly in the fall of 1922, he had second thoughts about Stalin. He could see how Stalin dominated the troika, how the troika dominated the Politburo, and how the Politburo dominated the party. Once Lenin had valued Stalin as a peasant who was particularly close to the common people and understood them. Now he concluded that "Stalin is too rude" and that this rendered him "intolerable in the office of general secretary."[6] He recommended that Stalin be removed from that position.

Joseph Stalin (right) worked with Vladimir Lenin (left) to establish a Communist government in Russia after the revolution in 1917. Stalin became a dictator of the Soviet Union after Lenin's death in 1924.

It was too late. Stalin had already consolidated his power. Lenin turned to Trotsky to depose Stalin, but Trotsky failed to act. The following year, when Lenin suffered a final stroke, Trotsky attacked Stalin. The attack backfired when Trotsky was accused of straying from the principles of Karl Marx, the nineteenth-century German philosopher whose works had set the guidelines for communism. Controlled by Stalin, the party condemned Trotsky "for factionalism and anti-Marxist deviation."[7] Stalin had effectively taken over the party and the nation.

ROBBERY AND REVOLUTION

How did he do it? The answer lies in the person Stalin was at this time, and how he got to be that person. His name describes him. *Stalin* means "man of steel." It was not his real name. He had been born Josif Visarionovich Djugashvili on December 21, 1879. He had adopted the name Stalin in 1912 to "symbolize a hardened personality."[8]

His personality had been growing harder from his beginnings in a two-room hut in the small Georgian village of Gori. At the age of five he almost died from smallpox. The disease left his face deeply and permanently pockmarked. His parents were poor. His father was a drunk who beat him, and then died in a barroom fight when Stalin was eleven years old. His mother could neither read nor write, but she struggled and sacrificed to enroll Stalin in the Russian Orthodox Church seminary in Tiflis, Georgia.

At the seminary Stalin acquired the habit of systematically filing things away in his mind. He developed a phenomenal memory and the ability to pigeonhole facts, statistics, and people. This would play an important role in his rise to power and his ability to wield it. What he did not embrace at the seminary was a belief in, or a love for, God.

This was the time when Stalin came to regard Russian Tsar Nicholas II's government as a "humiliating regime."[9] He became involved with student revolutionaries, and in 1899 he was expelled from the seminary. In 1901 he joined the Tiflis branch of the Russian Social Democratic Labour party, the organization that would evolve into the Communist party of the Soviet Union. Over the next two years Stalin became involved in various revolutionary activities, and in 1903, he was arrested and exiled to eastern Siberia.

"I hung around mostly with the criminals," Stalin would remember about his first Siberian exile.[10] He learned from them, and after his escape from Siberia in 1904, he began to put this knowledge to work. Back in his native district of Georgia, he organized bank robberies to finance the political activities of the revolutionary leader he was now pledged to follow: Vladimir Lenin.

Lenin met Stalin for the first time at a party gathering in Finland. He saw a man who police records would describe as "thin [with] thick black hair, a thin mustache but no beard, the marks of smallpox on his face, an oval head, a straight but not high forehead, arched eyebrows, sunken hazel eyes with a yellow tint, a straight nose." At 5 feet 4 inches (162 cm), he was as short as he was skinny. He "had a pointed chin, soft voice, a birthmark on his left ear . . . his left arm was withered, and . . . the second and third toes of his left foot had grown together." It was not a picture that suggested stature or leadership.[11] Nevertheless, Lenin found him a true representative of the downtrodden peasantry, a brave bandit who took action while the intellectuals talked endlessly, splitting hairs over revolutionary doctrine.

BACK TO SIBERIA

In June 1906, Stalin married Ekaterina Svanidze. A year later they had a son, Yakov. Shortly after the birth, however, Ekaterina contracted typhus and died. Stalin, who from all reports never revealed his feelings, broke down and sobbed uncontrollably with grief. It is believed that Ekaterina was the only person in his life that he ever truly loved.

Stalin pulled himself together. He left his son with his wife's sister and went to the Baku oil fields to work as a labor organizer. There he established soviets to confront the industrialists and the tsarist government, and eventually to serve as the organizing nucleus of the revolution. He was very successful in recruiting laborers from the peasant class for the soviets. Indeed, Stalin's understanding of peasants would prove key to the success of the coming revolution.

The party leadership took notice of his accomplishments. He was appointed to a four-man unit charged with organizing revolutionary activity in the far reaches of Russia. Although he was not considered an intellectual, because of his loyalty and peasant roots he was put in charge of producing the revolutionary underground newspaper *Pravda*. He became aware of the problems of organizing the many diverse ethnic groups of the Russian Empire for revolution. This led him to Vienna in 1913 to learn from Austrian Socialists how they went about unifying the various nationalities in the Austro-Hungarian Empire.

Upon his return to St. Petersburg, Stalin was arrested, and once again exiled to Siberia. He was still there when World War I broke out in 1914.

COMES THE REVOLUTION

It was March 1917 before Stalin was able to make his way back from Siberia to St. Petersburg. Much had happened in his absence. For one thing, the name of the city had been changed in 1914 to Petrograd. More important, Russia had been losing the war, the tsar had given up his throne, a Provisional Government had been established by a coalition of enlightened royalists and moderate socialists, and Lenin was expected to make a triumphal return to Russia after a seventeen-year absence.

Lenin's first act when he arrived was to proclaim the beginning of a "worldwide Socialist revolution."[12] He demanded that the Provisional Government place the Bolsheviks (the extreme left wing of the Russian Social Democratic Labour party) in charge in order to establish the "Dictatorship of the Proletariat"—meaning rule by the workers as determined by their radical leader, Vladimir Lenin.[13]

In July, following a Bolshevik march on the Provisional Government's headquarters in which Stalin participated, he, Lenin, and the other Bolshevik leaders were arrested and charged with "high treason and organizing an armed uprising."[14] As Lenin fled to Finland and Trotsky went to prison, Stalin went underground to organize the Bolsheviks for their next campaign to seize the government. In November 1917 it succeeded; the Provisional Government was overthrown, and the Bolsheviks were in power.

Stalin was appointed commissar of nationalities. This was an important stepping-stone for his future career. It put him in touch with Bolshevik leaders and the soviets—the workers' councils—throughout Russia. Names, activities, political views, ethnic loyalties, group allegiances, corruptibility, and personal strengths and flaws were all reduced to items placed in the neat filing cabinet that was Stalin's brain. Bolshevik doctrine was that the soviets would run the country, while the Bolsheviks provided the ideology by which it would be run. But Stalin recognized that both the members of the soviets and the Bolshevik thinkers could be influenced, manipulated, threatened, bribed, and eventually controlled. His experience as commissar of nationalities provided the first draft of the blueprint by which Stalin would come to power.

A SECOND MARRIAGE

Following the takeover of the government by the soviets, a counterrevolution erupted. Its forces were known as White Russians as opposed to the Bolshevik Red Russians. In June 1918 the Whites cut the supply route to the new Bolshevik capital of Moscow. Stalin was given the responsibility of overseeing the troops assigned by Lenin to reopen the supply route. Stalin's role in accomplishing that brought on a major confrontation with Trotsky, who was commissar of military affairs.

Stalin found that officers appointed by Trotsky were corrupt, so Stalin removed them. When Trotsky issued orders, Stalin told his officers to ignore them. Trotsky tried to persuade Lenin to court-martial Stalin, but Lenin refused. In the end, Stalin was regarded as the hero who saved Moscow, but in doing so he had made a lifelong enemy of Trotsky.

Because he was a hero, even though he didn't look the part, people were drawn to Stalin. Some women, particularly those committed to the Bolshevik ideal, viewed him as a romantic figure. One who was particularly attracted to him was Nadezhda Alliluyeva, the eighteen-year-old daughter of a loyal Bolshevik family. She was twenty-two years younger than the widowed Stalin, and he had known her since she was a child. Indeed, when Nadezhda was two years old, Stalin had fished her out of the Black Sea after she had fallen in, and may have saved her life.

From all accounts, Nadezhda worshiped the forty-year-old Stalin as a hero of the revolution. There is no way of knowing the nature or depth of Stalin's feelings toward her. He had been a widower for many years. He never would have admitted it, but perhaps he was lonely. Whatever the reason, in 1919 he married Nadezhda Alliluyeva.

Nadezhda would bear Stalin two children, Vasily and Svetlana. She also would become one of Lenin's secretaries, a connection that certainly didn't hurt Stalin's influence with the Russian dictator. It was, however, a stormy marriage, and it would end in tragedy.

STACKING THE SOVIETS

By November 1920 the Russian civil war was coming to an end. Stalin had fallen out of favor with Lenin because of disobeying orders during the war with Poland. Nevertheless, in April 1922, Lenin appointed Stalin general secretary of the Communist party. It was an important position and one that Stalin used cunningly to establish his influence over the soviets scattered throughout the land.

The soviets were supposed to be the ruling agencies. They would send representatives to the Central Committee to express their will. The Central Committee would consider the opinions and desires of the various soviets, debate and reconcile them, and pass them along to the Council of People's Commissars for action. The council was a sort of cabinet made up of heads of the various branches of government. Stalin was, of course, a member. Lenin was the council chairman, who appointed Stalin and the other members of the council. The ultimate power rested with him.

Stalin started his takeover effort from the bottom. He created a network of members of local soviets who were loyal to him. He spoke the language of the common man, convinced them that his goals should be their goals, distributed perks and gave them authority, and when all else failed, he bribed and threatened them. The result was that it was his choices who were elected to the Central Committee. Then, slowly but increasingly, he used the Central Committee to bend the Council of People's Commissars to his will. If there was a dispute, the Politburo was always under pressure by Stalin to settle it in his favor. With Lenin's death, he increased that pressure.

Stalin, Nikolai Bukharin, Lev Kamenev, and Grigori Zinoviev (left to right) were members of the Politburo, the political arm of the Communist Central Committee. As Stalin gained power, he removed his enemies from the Politburo and the Central Committee, usually by having them killed.

There would be opposition at every turn. It would come from the party's four most prominent leaders: Leon Trotsky, of course; Grigori Zinoviev and Lev Kamenev, who along with Stalin made up the ruling troika before and after Lenin's death; and Nikolai Bukharin, at first a friend and major supporter of Stalin's. They had all been fellow revolutionaries and former comrades of Stalin. Eventually, he would have all four of them killed.

CHAPTER TWO

THE NEW ECONOMIC POLICY

> **We have caught up with and outdistanced the advanced countries politically by having built the proletarian dictatorship. But this is not enough. We have to catch up with and outdistance the advanced countries also economically.**
>
> Speech by Joseph Stalin, November 19, 1928

The network of supporters Stalin created grew to become the bureaucracy that would run the government of the USSR as he wanted it run. Its first casualty was democracy within the Communist party itself. Stalin insisted, as had Lenin, that authority should be exercised by leadership from above. The job of those in the lower ranks was to see that the "correct line" was carried out.[1]

Trotsky challenged this. He demanded the removal from powerful party positions of "those who at the first voice of criticism, of objection, of protest" take action "for the purpose of repression." However, Trotsky was not being consistent. He had formerly approved of Lenin's rule banning splinter groups within the party. When Stalin cited this rule and lashed out at "democrats," Trotsky had to back off. Then Stalin played his trump card. He revealed an order, written by Lenin before his illness, that authorized the Central Committee "to expel its own members for creating factions." It was a threat aimed at Trotsky.[2]

THE ARROGANT TROTSKY

Trotsky and Stalin were the same age, forty-four, at the time of Lenin's death. Trotsky was an intellectual, skeptical of the ability of the common man to make decisions in his own best interest. He gave lip service to democracy, but had agreed with Lenin that the Bolshevik leadership knew what was best for the workers. When he opposed Stalin for imposing his will on the soviets, he was acting out of rivalry rather than conviction.

In the early days, Trotsky had only contempt for Stalin. He regarded him as a peasant, crude and unmannered, a mental lightweight. Later he saw him as dangerous, a bull in the china shop who acted on the sort of impulses that could destroy the revolution. Now, however, he feared Stalin, for it had dawned on Trotsky that behind the shambling, clumsy facade there was a mind as complex and devious as it was sinister.

Even recognizing this, Trotsky could not restrain his arrogance. He was brilliant, and he knew it, and this was his greatest failing. Often, even those who admired Trotsky did not really like him. He had done great things, but his cold and conceited attitude had cost him the support of many who might have been his friends. His greatest support came from those removed from him, rather than from those who were close. His charisma worked best at a distance.

Trotsky believed in "permanent revolution."[3] This meant extending the revolution in Russia to other countries. As a Marxist, Trotsky was loyal to Karl Marx's theory that the Socialist revolution must eventually be worldwide to succeed. Stalin deviated from this principle. He substituted the doctrine of "Socialism in one country."[4] Later, when Stalin ruled the USSR, the principle of exporting the revolution to the other countries of the world would be an on-again, off-again policy, but initially it was a major area of disagreement between Trotsky and Stalin.

INDEPENDENCE AND RECONQUEST

When Stalin came to power, the "one country" was a shambles. Before the revolution, tsarist Russia had been a vast empire made up of conquered territories. There were many non-Russian ethnic groups within its boundaries. Their inhabitants were loyal to what they considered to be their nation, rather than to the Russian Empire. When the Bolshevik government first took power, Lenin, together with Stalin, who was then commissar of nationalities, issued a "Declaration of the Rights of Peoples" for those national minorities that had been ruled by the tsar. The declaration said that every nation had a right to self-determination, and that this right included separation from the Soviet Union.

As a result, the former Russian Empire began to fall apart. Regional and ethnic loyalties quickly took precedence over enthusiasm for bolshevism. Finland, Poland, Lithuania, Latvia, and Estonia—all territories of Russia under the tsar—proclaimed their independence. The Ukraine splintered into independent Ukraine, Polish Ukraine, and—briefly—German-occupied Ukraine, Georgia, Armenia, and Azerbaijan formed the independent Transcaucasian Commissariat. Siberia declared its independence.

Lenin had acted quickly to reverse the Declaration of the Rights of Peoples. He dispatched Bolshevik armies to topple the new regimes. Stalin was instrumental in installing Communists loyal to him in their place. After 1922, when the Union of Soviet Socialist Republics (USSR) was established, Stalin's followers succeeded in having territories join the union as Socialist republics. However, even Lenin himself had been appalled by Stalin's "heavy-handed approach in forcing the non-Russian soviet republics to accept formal federation" with the USSR.[5] By the time Stalin replaced Lenin, the boundaries of the Soviet Union had been established and would define the nation until World War II broke out in 1939.

THE HARDSHIPS OF REFORM

In 1924 the USSR was made up of roughly the same territory as that of the former tsarist empire. Finland, Poland, Latvia, Lithuania, and Estonia were no longer included, but the Soviet Union still covered more land area—6,592,800 square miles (17,075,352 square km)—than any other country in the world. It stretched from the Baltic Sea, Barents Sea, and Bering Strait in the north to Iran, Afghanistan, and China in the south, and from the borders of Poland, Hungary, Romania, and the Black Sea in the west to the Bering Sea and the Sea of Japan in the east. It included the Russian Republic, most of Ukraine, Georgia, Kazakh, Belorussia, and Siberia, as well as other areas. It spanned the continents of Europe and Asia.

The population of the USSR at that time was approximately 147 million. Slightly more than 76 percent were peasants who worked the land.

Eight and a half percent of the people were landowners. Two and a half percent were white-collar workers, many of whom worked for various government departments at both the local and national level. Ten and a half percent of the citizens of the USSR were classified simply as "workers." Their jobs were in a variety of industries, many of them relatively new, ranging from the oil fields and the coal mines to factories and steel plants.

Under the tsar, the empire had lagged far behind the rest of Europe in the industrial revolution. At the beginning of the 1920s, the situation was even worse. According to Geoffrey Hosking, professor of Russian history at the University of London, 1921 manufacturing output was "a fifth or less of the 1913 level: in the case of iron and steel it was actually below 5 per cent."[6] Unemployment was high, and as new job seekers migrated from rural areas to the cities in search of work, it skyrocketed. Millions of former soldiers seeking jobs in industry pushed the unemployment figures to astronomical levels.

When unemployment is high, it is easy to keep wages low. The soviets, which were supposed to represent the workers, had been co-opted by the government. Any other labor unions were considered counterrevolutionary, and therefore against the law—just as they had been under the tsar. Meanwhile, in the industrial areas, there were massive housing shortages, a scarcity of food, and soaring food prices.

RELAXING THE RULES

Drought had drastically reduced crop output. Under communism, all land was owned by the state. The crops belonged to the state, which seized them. The peasants could not sell them. As a result, they had no incentive to grow more food than they could eat. A famine developed in the land. People starved to death.

In 1921, Lenin had instituted the New Economic Policy (NEP) to deal with this situation. When Stalin took over in 1924, the NEP was firmly in place. It was a retreat from communism, "a partial return to private enterprise."[7] The peasants no longer had to turn over their crops to the government. Instead, they paid a tax on what they produced, and were allowed to sell it at a profit. Although private property had technically been abolished,

Under the New Economic Policy (NEP), productive farmers, or kulaks, operated huge farms and hired peasants to work the land. In this photo taken during the late 1930s, women are going to work on a farm, owned collectively by the government, because white male peasants served in the army.

they could now own and run small farms. They could hire labor. Citizens could start new businesses. Badly managed industrial plants were returned to their former owners. The entire Communist financial system was reorganized along semicapitalist lines. Foreign capitalists were invited to invest in state-owned businesses. The response was limited.

By 1925 criticism of the NEP among workers was growing. The commissar for finance revealed that "the pay of miners, metal workers, and engine drivers was still lower than it had been before 1914." Housing shortages in industrial areas were acute with "families of six and seven people" forced to live "in one room." Workers resented "the peasants who charged them such high prices" for food. The Communist promise of worker control of factories and other workplaces was a buried dream.[8]

Nor was the NEP working particularly well for the peasants. It had done away with the idea of state-owned collectively worked farms, but the promise of peasants owning their own land had not been realized. The migration of the unemployed had been reversed, and thousands of former peasants had streamed back to the farmlands to claim a strip of land for their own under the NEP. But these farms were too small to provide a living for them. A sort of rat race developed in which former prosperous peasants had an edge. Because they were productive, the government had allowed them to keep their farms, and even to enlarge them. Now they were leasing other small farms and merging them. They hired the peasants they bought them from to work the land. A new class of landowners sprang up called kulaks.

THE KULAK QUESTION

Stalin's wide-ranging political machine exercised influence over who would, and who would not, succeed as a kulak. Just as he controlled the workers' soviets and selected managers—and sometimes owners—for factories, his local agents picked for kulaks those who would accumulate land in the far-flung agricultural regions of the USSR. These were men who would do his bidding, men with weaknesses for money, liquor, and sex. He appointed the party functionaries who often collaborated with the kulaks, and sometimes he personally decided who would control a large farm in a specific area.

The aim of the NEP was to produce food for the country. While it can't be called a failure, it was never quite the success it was hoped it would be. In 1913 grain production had been 81.6 million tons. The highest production under NEP was 76.8 million tons, reached in 1926. After that production fell off again. While the small group of kulaks prospered, the average peasant and his family were still struggling to make ends meet.

Inevitably, the NEP came under attack from Trotsky and others considered to be the left wing of the party. More surprising opposition came from Grigori Zinoviev and Lev Kamenev, the other two members of the troika headed by Stalin. They had supported the NEP since its inception, but in the summer of 1925 they attacked the policy as "a dangerous concession to . . . the kulaks." Actually, they were not so much concerned with the NEP as they were with exploiting "an issue on which they could mobilize opposition to the leadership" of Stalin. As members of the ruling troika, they had always been dominated by Stalin, but now it seemed that the worms had turned.[9]

ZINOVIEV AND KAMENEV

Originally, what bound the troika of Stalin, Zinoviev, and Kamenev together was their antagonism to Trotsky. This was particularly true of Zinoviev. Although he had sometimes differed with Lenin, Zinoviev had been Lenin's closest and most loyal supporter, following him into exile and then returning to Russia to stand by his side during and after the revolution. Trotsky, on the other hand, although widely regarded as Lenin's successor, had opposed him when the party split into factions, and had consistently alienated Zinoviev with his air of intellectual superiority.

Zinoviev, although a gifted public speaker, lacked leadership ability. He was not a man of strong will, nor was he always consistent in the positions he took. He was, however, invaluable as an organizer and an administrator. Throughout the chaos of revolution, civil war, and afterward, Zinoviev had created the infrastructure that enabled the new Communist government to function. Where Stalin had worked to create a political machine that would establish his personal power, Zinoviev had organized the paperwork, compiled the statistics, and divided the government into departments that could function in a practical manner.

He continued in this effort as a member of the troika. It was not in his nature to want to dominate as Lenin had. Because of this, he allowed himself to be dominated by Stalin. This was also true of Lev Kamenev, the third member of the troika.

Kamenev was Trotsky's brother-in-law, but they didn't get along. In the past Kamenev hadn't hesitated to join with Zinoviev and Stalin to keep Trotsky from seizing power. Like the others, he had been a member of the party from the beginning and was a respected revolutionary comrade. He was not a leader. However, he was influenced by Zinoviev, and by his dedication to Marxist principles, to conclude that the NEP was a betrayal of communism.

THE NEP PREVAILS

The situation of the proletariat—the working class—became an issue at the Fourteenth Party Congress in December 1925. The congress was a large, unwieldy body elected by local party organizations to debate policy issues. Many of its members were controlled by Stalin, and any recommendations of the congress were subject to approval by the Politburo.

Despite these obstacles, Zinoviev and Kamenev led a faction at the congress accusing the Stalinist leadership of "favoring the kulaks at the expense of the proletariat, pursuing a policy of state capitalism, not socialism . . . and turning the dictatorship of the proletariat into a dictatorship over the proletariat." They were immediately accused of launching an "attack on socialism" revealing a "lack of faith in the Russian people's ability to create a socialist society." Stalin's powerful ally Nikolai Ivanovich Bukharin led this response to the Zinoviev-Kamenev charges.[10]

Bukharin was the author of *Political Economy of the Leisure Class*, a classic work of Communist theory, as well as other books. He was the editor of *Pravda*, the official party newspaper, and of the *Great Soviet Encyclopedia*. He had been imprisoned in Siberia, fought in the revolution, was chairman of the Comintern (the Communist International organization pledged to world revolution), and was a member of the Central Committee. Because of his reputation as a dedicated Communist with unquestioned integrity, his support of the New Economic Policy carried great weight.

Stalin and Bukharin prevailed. Kamenev kept shouting, "We are against the theory of one-man rule" to no avail. The NEP policy remained in place by a vote in the congress of 539 to 65. Kamenev was dismissed from his government post and was no longer a member of the ruling troika. Zinoviev remained, but no longer had any power. In effect, the troika was dissolved and the one-man dictatorship of Joseph Stalin was established.

OUSTING THE OPPOSITION

However, the challenge to Stalin wasn't over. Trotsky had stayed aloof from the debate. Past conflicts with Zinoviev and Kamenev had made him reluctant to side with them. After all, Stalin was in power rather than Trotsky in large part because of their support. Nevertheless, by the spring of 1926, "Trotsky, Zinoviev and Kamenev at last recognized their common interest in challenging Stalin, and succeeded in creating a united opposition." In July this resulted in the "Declaration of the Thirteen," which spelled out the case against Stalin's leadership and the NEP. The main demand was "a curb on the menace to socialism represented by the growing wealth of the . . . kulaks."[11]

This time the countercharge was that Trotsky, Zinoviev, and Kamenev were organizing a "conspiracy against the party." This was a most serious accusation since all three served on the Politburo. Aroused by Bukharin with Stalin's backing, the Central Committee expelled Zinoviev from the Politburo and deprived him of all his government posts. Trotsky exploded. Nose to nose with Stalin, he called him the "grave digger of the revolution." The next day the Central Committee deprived Trotsky and Kamenev of their seats on the Politburo.[12]

Despite being out of power, the three men continued their opposition to the NEP. Trotsky, in particular, arrogant as always, could not hold his tongue. Finally, in December 1927, all three were thrown out of the Communist party. Zinoviev and Kamenev petitioned for readmission, but were told they would have to reapply in six months. Trotsky kept agitating.

In January 1928, Trotsky was arrested by Stalin's secret police and exiled to the farthest frontier of Soviet Central Asia. From there he would wander the world, its foremost anti-Stalinist. He would never return to the Union of Soviet Socialist Republics, the Communist empire he had played such a major role in creating.

CHAPTER THREE

THE SECRET POLICE

> **We are exterminating the bourgeoisie as a class. During the investigation, do not look for evidence that the accused acted in deed or word against soviet power. The first questions that you ought to put are: To what class does he belong? What is his origin? What is his education or profession? And it is these questions that ought to determine the fate of the accused. In this lies the significance and essence of the Red Terror.**
>
> Martyn Ivanovich Latsis, eastern district chairman of the Cheka (secret police)

The key to Stalin's grip on the Soviet Union was the cult of personality, which let him merge himself and his policies with the identity of the nation. It stemmed from his ability to manipulate the people as well as their government and its policies and programs. Essential to this, however, was a legal terrorist organization with the power to brutally enforce Stalin's will: the secret police.

THE CHEKA

For centuries the tsars of Russia had controlled their subjects with a secret-police organization authorized to probe into every aspect of life, and to punish those suspected of antigovernment activity with the harshest measures. On December 7, 1917, one month after the Bolsheviks took control of the government, the tsarist tradition was echoed by the establishment of the Extraordinary Commission for Struggle with Counterrevolution and Sabotage. Known as the Cheka, it was the first Soviet secret-police organization.

It was headed by Feliks Edmundovich Dzerzhinsky, a Pole who had been active in revolutionary activities in Poland and Russia for twenty-two years. Dzerzhinsky was a fanatic and an executioner. He regarded himself as

Feliks Edmundovich Dzerzhinsky founded the Soviet secret police, the Cheka, in 1917 under Lenin's orders. The Cheka acted as the government's eyes and ears, often gathering evidence against, or even executing, enemies of the state.

the "avenging sword" of the proletariat, acting on Lenin's demand for "a purge of the Russian land from all vermin . . . the idle rich, priests, bureaucrats, and slovenly and hysterical intellectuals."[1] Estimates of those murdered by the Cheka between 1917 and 1923 range as high as 200,000 people.

In 1922 the Cheka was reorganized as the Unified State Political Administration (OGPU; sometimes known simply as the GPU). Still basically the secret police, under Dzerzhinsky it served Stalin's rapidly expanding party machine. Although Lenin was still alive, Stalin's organization was already beginning to be recognized as a major factor in government control. Behind his back, Stalin was called *"Tovarishch Kartotekov*—Comrade Card-Index."[2] He was soon providing the data in that index to the OGPU for action against his opponents.

THE FIRST "SHOW TRIAL"

When Dzerzhinsky died in 1926 at the age of forty-eight, there were rumors of foul play. These were never proved, and were probably only a legacy of the violence by which he had lived. He was succeeded as head of the OGPU by Vyacheslav Menzhinsky, a very different sort of secret-police administrator.

Menzhinsky was not a public figure. He was not well known outside of the counterintelligence service and certain political circles close to Stalin. He was most comfortable working behind the scenes. As ruthless as Dzerzhinsky had been, Menzhinsky ran his department with far more secrecy, and in many ways was more efficient and more deadly.

Acting on Stalin's orders, it was Menzhinsky whose agents had driven Trotsky into exile at the beginning of 1928. By that time the OGPU organization was beginning a major transformation. It would no longer be merely a secret-police force bent on gathering intelligence, raiding antigovernment meetings, planting informants, and sometimes torturing and murdering dissidents. Under Stalin it was assuming more and more duties, building greater power, turning itself into a military force with which any opposition would have to reckon.

The OGPU would handle the "administration of corrective labour camps" where political prisoners as well as criminals were held. It would be granted "judicial powers" in addition to its "broad investigative" powers. It would have "a monopoly on police functions." Finally, it would have "its own army, with aviation and tank units, and a vast network of spies and informers in factories, government offices and army units." It would be the club with which Stalin beat the nation into submission.[3]

An early example of this designed to impress both the Soviet public and world opinion was the first of the so-called show trials held in Moscow in March 1928. Managed by the OGPU, Stalin set the mood: "We have internal enemies," he proclaimed. "We have external enemies. This, comrades, must not be forgotten for a single moment."[4]

There was OGPU involvement at every level of the trial. They had arrested the fifty-five persons charged with plotting to sabotage a major industrial complex, the Shakhty mines in the Donets Basin. Through either brainwashing or torture, or both, they had extracted confessions from most of those accused. In courts controlled by the OGPU, eleven were sentenced to death. Six of the sentences were reduced; five of the condemned were executed.

DISCARDING BUKHARIN

Stalin also would use the OGPU to enforce the about-face policy, which followed his defeat of Trotsky, Zinoviev, and Kamenev. With Bukharin's strong support, Stalin had championed the modified capitalism of the NEP. His opponents had wanted collectivization—ownership and management by the people of the land, resources, produce, and factories of the nation. Now that he had won, Stalin completely reversed his position.

At the end of May 1928, Stalin proclaimed "the collectivization of agriculture and the rapid development of heavy industry."[5] He had not formally declared the end of the NEP, but in effect he had repealed it. Collectivization would not be gradual and voluntary. It would be immediate and backed up by the full force of the OGPU. It would be "a sharp break with the past" of the NEP.[6]

Bukharin was shocked. He felt betrayed. He had provided Stalin with the carefully reasoned arguments in support of the NEP. He had helped drive its opponents out of the Communist party. He had done all this out of a conviction he assumed Stalin shared. Now he saw Stalin as a man with no convictions, and told him so. To his face, Bukharin called Stalin "a petty Oriental despot."[7]

Out of desperation, Bukharin met with his old anti-NEP opponent Kamenev. "The revolution is ruined," he told Kamenev. Inevitably, the OGPU made Stalin aware of the meeting. Stalin accused Bukharin of "seeking an alliance with the Trotskyists." Throughout 1929, as the NEP was being dismantled, Bukharin was increasingly isolated by Stalin.[8] He became regarded as a party traitor afflicted with "political syphilis."[9]

On November 17, 1929, Bukharin was removed from the Politburo. Those in the party who had sided with him also were ostracized. Along with Bukharin, they took back what they said. They wrote the Central Committee that it had been "right in this dispute. Our views have turned out to be erroneous. Recognizing our errors, we shall conduct a decisive struggle against all deviations from the party's general line . . . ."[10]

Bukharin and the others were dedicated Communists. Was exclusion from the party to which they had dedicated their lives simply too much for them to bear? Had they really convinced themselves that they had been in error? Or did they sense that expulsion was but the first step leading to their liquidation? Such confessions of error, crime, treason, and espionage would be common in the USSR during the decade that followed.

THE COLLECTIVIZATION POLICY

The first "extraordinary measures" against the NEP "to secure the forced requisitioning of grain" were authorized by the Central Committee under pressure from Stalin in 1928.[11] By then the kulaks were producing a significant part of the USSR's agricultural output. In order to keep the price up, they were withholding grain from the markets. As a result, there were again food shortages throughout the nation.

Stalin had in the past empowered many of these kulaks as a way of establishing his influence and control over the vast rural areas of the country. They were part of the network the OGPU supervised in the service of the dictator. Now, however, they had served their purpose, and Stalin was making them the scapegoats justifying the abandonment of the NEP. Over the years he had seen to it that local officials in farm regions were appointed by him. Oversight by the OGPU ensured their loyalty. Now he called on these officials "to use force and make the kulaks surrender the grain." He urged "poorer peasants to inform against their better off neighbors," assuring them that "a quarter of the grain confiscated was to be sold to them at low prices." He called for criminal prosecution of anyone who did not cooperate. Finally he spoke the chilling words that spelled out the fate of the kulaks: "There will be sabotage of grain procurements as long as the kulak exists."[12]

By eliminating the kulaks, Stalin was destroying the most productive farmers. This was necessary in order to put the USSR back on the track to fundamental communism, which called for collective ownership of the land. Stalin spelled it out: "[We] must steadfastly unify the least productive individual peasant holdings into collective farms."[13] According to British historian Lord Alan Bullock, this "marked the opening of one of the most tragic chapters in the history of Russia: the collectivization of Soviet agriculture."[14]

"DEKULAKIZATION"

The word coined for the liquidation of the kulaks was "dekulakization."[15] It was misleading. Stalin's program of collectivization in the late 1920s and early 1930s swept up and destroyed many peasants and their families who had never come close to attaining kulak status. Farms, homes, and other property were confiscated by the state in the process of creating large state-owned and state-run agricultural cooperatives. While kulaks were banned from the farming co-ops, hundreds of thousands of families were transported to remote areas to work on collective farms under conditions little better than that of the serfs in tsarist Russia. Under OGPU enforcement, resisters were shot or hanged.

Stalin fully recognized the extent of the horror, but considered it necessary. Many years later, in a conversation with Prime Minister Winston Churchill of Great Britain, he explained why. "The Collective Farm policy was a terrible struggle," he said. "Ten millions. It was fearful. Four years it lasted. It was absolutely necessary for Russia, if we were to avoid periodic famines, to plough the land with tractors. . . . When we gave tractors to the peasants, they were all spoiled in a few months. Only Collective Farms with workshops could handle tractors. . . . he [the kulak] does not want the Collective Farm and would rather do without the tractors . . . the great bulk [of kulaks] were wiped out by their labourers."[16]

Industrial workers as well as peasants were victims of the policies of collectivization. Food distribution to workers in nonfarming areas was reorganized by the Central Committee according to Stalin's design. The NEP bureaucracy was accused of being "clogged with anti-Soviet agents, forty-eight of whom were shot recently."[17] Admitting that Russia had a labor problem, the Central Committee ruled that a person would have to prove that he was a worker in a government-authorized factory or business in order to obtain food. If one didn't work, one didn't eat.

THE FIRST FIVE-YEAR PLAN

Harsh discipline of workers was regarded by Stalin as essential to building up Soviet industry, which lagged far behind the countries of Europe and the United States. There was fear that the capitalist countries might act to overthrow the world's first Communist government. Their factories were capable of turning out arms and munitions far more efficiently and quickly and in greater quantities than the Soviet Union could. Also, products—everything from mule harnesses and stoves to tractors and medical equipment—had to be produced for the peasants who were providing the food. The need was urgent, and in November 1928 it was met with the adoption of the first Five-Year Plan.

Actually, the first Five-Year Plan lasted only four years, the claim that it had met its goals being made in December 1932. By then the industrial force had more than doubled to ten million workers. The production of raw materials—coal, oil, iron ore, and pig iron—needed to fire up industry had also approximately doubled. There had been considerable growth in heavy industry, particularly in the production of machine tools. These tools provided the foundation for new factories producing weapons for the nation's military defense, as well as new kinds of products. Huge tractor factories were built for the collectives, which by 1932 were approaching the Five-Year Plan goal of 85 percent of farmlands.

At the same time, the first Five-Year Plan had neglected basic human needs. The textile industry fell into decline; clothes were of poor quality and in short supply. The railroads—always a problem because of the immense distances in the USSR—were neglected; food spoiled before it could be shipped; manufactured goods lay on sidings rusting in the snows of winter. New housing was rarely built, and crowded living conditions prevailed, with many families forced into unheated shacks and other hovels.

A main legacy of the first Five-Year Plan was a management structure that became an important part of the Stalin political machine. People's commissariats had been created to administer the various branches of industry. They set production goals and appointed the managers charged with reaching them. Overfulfillment of the goals was rewarded; underfulfillment might be punished. Worker safety was rarely a consideration.

To succeed, a factory manager had to be able to get his hands on the raw materials—coal, oil, and more—to run his plant. This could involve bribes, favors, even violence. Goods were stolen; trucks were hijacked; entire trainloads of supplies were ambushed and rerouted. The competition was more fierce than among the most ambitious capitalist competitors. Stalin played the top men off one against another, and they played their subordinates off one against another. Those who failed him were dismissed in disgrace. Sometimes they were even arrested and charged with sabotage.

THE TYRANT AS HUSBAND

Even as the list of victims widened, the plight of the forcibly collectivized peasants was clearly defining Stalin as a tyrant. People high and low feared him too much to protest, but there was a murmur throughout the land that a despot as evil as the tsars was back in charge. Revulsion at what was being done by his edicts even reached inside his home.

Nadezhda, Stalin's young second wife and the mother of two of his three children, had enrolled at the Industrial Academy to study synthetic fibers. A committed party activist, she considered it her duty to play an active role in the technical development of the nation. From fellow students at the academy, she learned what was happening as peasants in the Ukraine were being collectivized.

Stalin's second wife, Nadezhda Alliluyeva, with their daughter, Svetlana Alliluyeva Stalin

Throughout her marriage, Nadezhda had idolized her husband. Recently, however, she had become troubled by the effects on him of the power and privilege he had amassed. His former facade of peasant humility had slipped away, revealing a naked arrogance. Subordinates cringed before it, and his arrogance was present in his dealings with his children and his wife as well. Whatever else Stalin was, he was not a sensitive man; he was not a man who hesitated to ride roughshod over the feelings of those who should have been closest to him.

When Nadezhda gently reproached him for the effect of his policies on the peasants in the Ukraine, Stalin answered with withering sarcasm. As relations between them became more strained, she took the children and left him. However, she returned. Still Stalin displayed contempt toward her and her views in both private and public. Things came to a head on November 8, 1932, at a party in the Kremlin in Moscow.

THE LAST WORD

In front of the assembled guests, Stalin and Nadezhda had a quarrel. Both stormed out of the room. Stalin went to his quarters. Nadezhda, distraught, strolled around the Kremlin courtyard in the winter night with a friend. Finally she left the friend and went to her room. The next morning, when the housekeeper went to wake her, she found Nadezhda lying dead with a pistol beside her. She was thirty-one years old.

There were whispers that she might have been murdered, but the rumors had no real substance. All the evidence confirmed that it was a suicide. It has been claimed that there was a suicide note, but if so it was suppressed. When Stalin was informed, he appeared shaken. His emotion may have been not so much grief, however, as rage.

He did not attend Nadezhda's funeral, nor her memorial service. He never visited her grave. Stalin did, however, go to view her open coffin at some point before the funeral. He stood before it for a moment, and then made an abrupt motion with his hand as if to dismiss it. Then, turning to leave, Stalin spoke his feelings toward Nadezhda: "She left me as an enemy!" he said.[18]

CHAPTER FOUR

EXPORTING COMMUNISM

In short, the Communists everywhere support every revolutionary movement against the existing social and political order of things.

Karl Marx and Friedrich Engels in *The Communist Manifesto*

"Socialism in one country" was the Stalin policy that broke with the Marxist principle of "world revolution" championed by Trotsky.[1] That principle had first been established by Karl Marx at a meeting of leftist party representatives in London in 1864. The organization they founded became known as The First International. In 1876, The First International fell apart after a series of quarrels among various representatives over methods and goals. In 1889, The Second International was founded in Paris. It collapsed when World War I nationalism and patriotism saw workers fighting overwhelmingly for their native lands rather than for world revolution.

On March 2, 1919, a meeting in Moscow of fifty-two delegates from a variety of countries was chaired by a five-member steering committee, which included Lenin. It established The Third International with the stated aim of promoting world revolution. Dominated by Soviet Russians, The Third International became known as the Comintern.

THE COMINTERN

Under Stalin the Comintern backed away from world revolution. It "functioned chiefly as an organ of Soviet control over the Communist movement" around the world.[2] However, the policy was not consistent. In general, and in varying degrees, between the time that Stalin assumed power and the start of World War II, the Comintern supported insurgent movements in other countries.

Mostly, in keeping with the policy of "Socialism in one country," that support was a matter of propaganda and diplomacy. Stalin could not afford to be seen as using the Comintern to take action for the Trotsky position of world revolution. He could not hang back, however, when a revolution against ruling warlords raised hopes for establishing a Communist state in China.

Two rival forces were battling the warlords and struggling to unify that country. One was the Chinese Communist party (CCP) formed in 1921. The other was the Kuomintang (KMT), the nationalist party led by former president of the Chinese Republic Sun Yat-sen.

SUPPORT FOR THE KUOMINTANG

The Comintern dispatched an agent to Shanghai to look into the strength of the CCP. While he was there, a seamen's strike organized by the Kuomintang broke out in Canton and Hong Kong. The KMT was behind a Chinese trade-union movement. When the agent reported back to Moscow, the Comintern concluded that the KMT had many more members, was better organized, and was more efficiently led than the Chinese Communist party. A decision was made to support the Kuomintang. Chinese Communists, acting on Soviet Comintern orders, would infiltrate the KMT and eventually take control of it.

Sun Yat-sen gladly accepted financing and armaments from the Comintern. His newly appointed chief of staff, Chiang Kai-shek, headed a delegation to Moscow to seek military support. When Chiang returned, he headed the reorganization of the Kuomintang "along Leninist lines."[3] However, after the death of Sun Yat-sen in March 1925, Chiang Kai-shek became the leader of the KMT, and set out to purge it of Communist influence.

Chiang Kai-shek and his horse, Black Dragon, in 1935

THE ADAPTABLE CHIANG

Born in Chekiang Province, China, in 1887, Chiang Kai-shek was the son of a salt merchant and his third wife. Chiang decided on a military career in his teens and received training in both Japan and China. In 1911, he fought in the revolution that brought Sun Yat-sen to power.

In 1917, Chiang followed Sun Yat-sen to Canton where Sun established an alliance with a local warlord. This led Chiang into involvement with the Green Gang, "a secret society that wielded great power in the Shanghai underworld." Through them, Chiang "engaged in financial speculation." There would always be rumors—unconfirmed—that he had amassed a fortune.[4]

Chiang was a party to the agreement reached on January 26, 1923, between the Comintern and the Kuomintang. It recognized that "conditions did not exist in China either for Communism or for a Soviet system." However, "there was a clear understanding . . . that the KMT would let the Soviet Comintern agents reorganize the party on Communist lines."[5] This pulled the rug out from under the Chinese Communist party and firmly allied the Comintern with Sun Yat-sen and Chiang.

The Comintern sent agent Michael Borodin to work with Chiang to reorganize the Kuomintang. By January 1924 the Kuomintang "had a Central Executive Committee that met every two months, and a small Standing Committee (equivalent to the Soviet Politburo)." A constitution, "drafted by Borodin, on orders from the Comintern," was adopted.[6]

THE ANTI-COMMUNIST CHIANG

Borodin supported the takeover of the KMT by Chiang after Sun Yat-sen's death. A year later, however, Chiang turned on him. Beginning in March 1926, "Chiang jailed alleged Soviet and Chinese Communist conspirators. He also purged high party posts of leading Communists, including the acting head of the propaganda department, Mao Tse-tung"—the future all-powerful chairman of the government of Communist China.[7]

Chiang led his forces northward, pushing the bands of various warlords from their territories, and eventually occupying Shanghai. In April

1927, Chiang instituted a "party purification" movement against Communists and their sympathizers in Shanghai and other areas.[8] In particular, he targeted the labor unions. When the Chinese Communist party, now allied with the Comintern, rallied to oppose him, Chiang formed an alliance with a powerful warlord, Feng Yu-hsiang. Together they forced the CCP forces to retreat.

During the next decade, China suffered constant warfare involving the Kuomintang, the CCP, area warlords, and Japanese invaders. Following Chiang's defeat of the Communists, the Comintern drew back from further involvement in China. It had backed the wrong horse, the Kuomintang. As a result, there would always be strained relations between the Chinese Communist party and the Soviet Comintern.

REDS IN VIETNAM

By 1930, with Trotsky, Zinoviev, Kamenev, and Bukharin all removed from government, Stalin could afford to co-opt their arguments and implement their policies as his own. "Socialism in one country" had faded from the public mind. There were too many foreign-policy considerations to stir up world revolution, but selective support of radical movements by the Comintern with Stalin's approval was definitely an option.

Acting on this option, the Comintern organized the Communist party of Indochina. Its self-appointed leader was Ho Chi Minh. On September 12, 1930, some six thousand members of the new party, most of them peasants, attacked their landlords in the French colony of Vietnam.

From the Comintern's viewpoint it was a classic situation. The French had seized Vietnam and taken over the land from the native population. Large landowners had then exploited the labor of the Vietnamese peasants to make the land productive and turn a gratifying profit. When the French army brutally put down the uprising, the picture was complete. "Hundreds of militants were arrested, and most of them were executed."[9] Comparisons to the Russian Revolution were not hard to make.

Ho fled to Hong Kong, where British authorities jailed him for two years. Released in 1933, he went to Moscow, where he received specialized training in revolutionary techniques at the Lenin Institute. He would return to Vietnam to organize resistance to the Japanese invasion during World War II, and after the war he would lead the fight for the liberation of Vietnam from French rule. By the time the French left and the United States sent troops to support anti-Communist Vietnamese forces in the 1960s, support for the Vietnam Communists by the Comintern had been in place for more than thirty years.

THE SPANISH CIVIL WAR

Of all the Comintern's foreign involvements, none was so extensive nor so effective propaganda-wise as its role in Spain in the 1930s. In December 1933, the Comintern set a new policy known as the "Popular Front."[10] It urged coalitions between Communists and other groups to effectively oppose rightist and centrist forces. In Spain, political parties ranging from democratic and liberal to Socialist and radical joined together to form the Spanish Popular Front. In February 1936, the Popular Front won a narrow victory in the elections and became the republican government of Spain.

On July 17, 1936, troops led by General Francisco Franco rebelled against the Popular Front government. It was the start of the Spanish Civil War. Known as the Falange, the rebels were right wing and strongly anti-Communist. They made no distinction among supporters of the Popular Front, many of whom were not Communists. The republican government had restricted many of the privileges of the church in Catholic Spain, and so the Falange had strong support from the church.

In other countries there was sympathy for both sides in the Spanish Civil War. Many people viewed the Spanish republican government as the instrument of reform. Many Catholics regarded it as a godless persecutor of the church.

General Franco appealed to Premier Benito Mussolini of Italy for help. Mussolini provided him with a dozen warplanes. Franco then approached the dictator of Germany, Adolf Hitler. He provided six more fighter planes. With this support, Franco's 15,000-man army crossed the Straits of Gibraltar from Morocco and invaded the Spanish mainland. The USSR responded by sending arms and military advisers to shore up the government.

As the fighting heated up, Germany and Italy became more deeply involved on the side of Franco. Italy sent ground troops, tanks, and artillery to back up his forces. Germany supplied him with the Condor Legion, a hundred combat planes flown by German and Spanish pilots. On April 26, 1937, the bombing and strafing of civilians in Guernica by German warplanes outraged public opinion around the world.

The tanks, arms, and aircraft the Soviets supplied were key to the republic's survival. The Comintern organized International Brigades to fight alongside the Spanish loyalists. In the United States, 2,800 volunteers—idealists who ranged from dedicated Socialists to naive anti-Fascists—were recruited for the Abraham Lincoln Brigade to fight against the Falange in Spain. In March 1937, the International Brigades defeated an Italian army corps at Guadalajara.

LA PASIONARIA

While the fighting was going on, the Spanish Communist party was increasingly dominating the Popular Front government thanks to the Comintern's role in the supply of arms from the Soviet Union. Communists organized and controlled the republican military. However, resistance was building to Communist control among non-Communist members of the republican government. Soon a devastating split developed between pro- and anti-Communist officials.

In the face of this, a key person who set the tone of unity against the Falange was Dolores Ibarurri. Known as *"La Pasionaria"* for her fervent devotion to the Communist cause, Ibarurri nevertheless had a "talent for organizing people of diverse backgrounds and ideologies to unite in a common cause." A leader of the Communists in government, she had gone on the radio during the siege of Madrid and rallied the people with the words *"No pasaran!"*—they shall not pass! Civilians rushed to the barricades, and the Falange was prevented from entering the city.[11]

Dolores Ibarurri was born in 1895, the eighth of eleven children All the men in her family worked from dawn to dusk in the mines. "That was our life," she would remember, "a deep pit without horizons."[12] She married a

General Francisco Franco led the right-wing rebel group the Falange in overthrowing the Soviet-sponsored Spanish government. Pictured in 1936, Franco served as dictator of Spain until 1975.

miner and had six children, four of whom she outlived. Marriage did not change her life. Hardship, illness, and hunger were always its hallmarks.

Convinced that there had to be a better system than the one she had always known, Ibarurri began reading Marxist literature. She joined the Spanish Communist party. In 1930, at the age of thirty-five, she was elected to its Central Committee. She was soon a leading party spokesperson. When the Falange struck in 1936, *La Pasionaria* rallied the republican opposition with her speeches over Radio Madrid. "It is better to die on your feet than to live on your knees!" she told the people, and they responded.[13]

As popular as she was, Ibarurri could not hold the coalition of the Popular Front together. On March 7, 1939, a vicious battle broke out in Madrid between Communists and anti-Communists. People were literally forced to take sides. Ibarurri was, of course, a Communist. When the fighting made it possible for the Falange to capture the city, she was forced to flee to the Soviet Union, where she remained for the next thirty-eight years. Before she left, *La Pasionaria* bid farewell to the International Brigades in a moving speech, which called them "the heroic example of democracy's solidarity and universality."[14] Actually, they owed their existence to the antidemocratic Comintern, which had failed once again to spark world revolution in a country other than the Soviet Union.

THE AMERICAN COMMUNIST PARTY

The Spanish Civil War is often regarded as a sort of training ground for World War II. German, Italian, and Russian military forces were all able to try out strategies, tactics, and weapons. The non-Spaniards who fought in Spain would be the seasoned troops who fought in the early battles of World War II.

In the mid-1930s, however, World War II was still in the future. In the United States, the possibility of war was not yet a major concern. The country was focused on the Great Depression in which, as President Franklin D. Roosevelt put it, "I see one-third of a nation ill-housed, ill-clad, ill-nourished."[15] In 1932, when Roosevelt was elected president, "one out of every four U.S. workers was unemployed."[16] Jobless World War I veterans were selling apples on street corners and lining up for meals at soup kitchens. Families who could not pay their rent were thrown out on the street and ended up living in tar-paper shacks with tin roofs. Farmers lost their land to drought, to tornadoes, and, when they couldn't pay their loans, to banks. Along with wives and children, they became migrant workers, heading for California to pick crops, only to be met at the state border by police, who turned many of them away. When Roosevelt assumed office, he launched the New Deal, a series of programs "aimed mainly at stabilizing the economy, and secondly at giving enough help to the lower classes to keep them from turning a rebellion into a real revolution."[17]

There will always be disagreement as to just how much support the Comintern provided, or was willing to provide, to encourage revolution in the United States in the 1930s. It was restricted by other Soviet foreign-policy commitments. After the Bolshevik revolution, the United States had refused to recognize the USSR. However, fifteen years later, on November 17, 1933, the Roosevelt government recognized the Soviet Union, and relations between the two countries were normalized. Russia now could buy much-needed machinery from the United States, and manufacturing this machinery would create much-needed jobs in the United States. Key to the agreement were Soviet "promises not to disseminate Communist propaganda in America."[18]

Nevertheless, there was a Communist party in the United States, and there was no law against its existence. During the depression years, it followed the Popular-Front policy and lent its support to labor unions, reform groups, and protest movements. However, it wasn't always successful in allying itself with other left-wing groups. The American Federation of Labor (AFL) successfully fought against Communist infiltration. The Socialist party condemned communism. The small band of anti-Stalinist followers of Trotsky that had organized in New York and other cities also denounced the Communist party.

The United States Communist party was small. By allying itself with the underdog, it attracted the support of many people who were not Communists, but who were sympathetic to the causes the party championed. These supporters would be labeled "fellow travelers," and many of them would one day have to answer for their involvement with the party.

The causes may have been just, but the company they kept would be highly suspect.

At its height in the 1930s, "the actual membership of the Communist Party was not large—fewer than 100,000 probably."[19] By the end of the decade its membership was far less than that. Nevertheless, throughout the period there was an effort by big business, and some law-enforcement groups, to label as Communist everything from sit-down strikes and anti-lynching protests to prison-reform movements and New Deal projects like the Works Progress Administration (WPA). The president was accused of being a Communist sympathizer, and his wife, Eleanor Roosevelt, was even accused of being a party member. To belong to the American Civil Liberties Union (ACLU), the National Association for the Advancement of Colored People (NAACP), the Amalgamated Clothing and Textile Workers Union (ACTWU), or any one of a number of other such groups was to risk being accused of being a Communist. Many innocent people were unjustly accused.

Not everybody was innocent. However, many of those who joined the party, or who simply supported one or another of its campaigns, backed off in horror when the Soviet Union signed a nonaggression pact with Germany in August 1939. Any influence the American Communist party had was all but gone when Germany and the USSR attacked Poland a month later. Whatever secret involvement the Comintern actually had in the American Communist party of the 1930s, its success can be measured in terms of the fear of communism it aroused in the United States, and in the legacy of paranoia that blossomed following World War II. But at establishing a revolutionary force in the United States, the Comintern was a failure.

CHAPTER FIVE

THE GREAT PURGES

All is in vain: the soul is blinded,
We are destined for the worms and maggots,
And not even the ashes remain
In the land of Russian justice.

Zinaida Gippius, Russian antirevolutionary poet

On December 1, 1934, Sergei Mironovich Kirov, the Politburo member regarded as Stalin's "second in command," was walking down a narrow corridor toward his office in the Smolny Institute in Leningrad (formerly Petrograd, originally St. Petersburg).[1] He was in a good mood. Two days earlier he had made an announcement to the citizens of Leningrad that the rationing of bread and other food would be ended. The people had cheered him; his popularity was at its height. Stalin referred to him as a "friend and beloved brother."[2]

As Kirov walked down the passageway, he saw a rather ordinary man approaching him. The man was Leonid Vasilyevich Nikolaev. He was a discharged employee of the Leningrad Workers' and Peasants' Inspectorate. As Kirov reached the door of his office, Nikolaev pulled out a revolver. He fired two shots. Kirov fell to the floor. Nikolaev then fainted, dropping beside his dying victim. People came running. It was too late. Kirov soon was dead.

His slaying was one of many such killings that took place in the USSR during that era. Nevertheless, this particular assassination had far-reaching effects unlike any other. Robert Conquest of the Hoover Institution at Stanford University concludes that "as an individual murder, there is, for various reasons, none to match the Kirov case." He views it as "the central justification for the whole theory of Stalinism and the necessity for endless terror," which marked the purges that followed.[3]

THE VICTIM

Sergei Mironovich Kirov was born in 1886 in a small town in northern Russia. His father was a drunkard who abandoned his family. When his mother died soon after, Sergei was raised partly by his grandmother and grew up partly in a local orphanage. In his teens, he went to a vocational school in the city of Kazan. There he became involved in radical politics.

He moved on to the Siberian city of Tomsk, and at the age of nineteen he joined the Social Democratic Labour party. Soon after, Kirov pushed his way into a dinner for liberal politicians, and forced them at gunpoint to listen to Social Democratic speakers. By 1905 he was smuggling guns for revolutionaries. In 1906 he was arrested and jailed for three years.

In 1912, when the Social Democratic party officially split, Kirov sided with Lenin and the Bolsheviks against the Mensheviks. After the successful takeover of the Russian government by the Bolsheviks in 1917, he was appointed head of the Military Revolutionary Committee in Astrakhan. His job was to bring the vast area of Caucasus into the Bolshevik fold. It involved putting down an uprising of anti-Bolshevik workers.

Kirov became a member of the Central Committee of the Communist party in 1922. In 1926 he supported Stalin's ouster of Zinoviev and Kamenev from the Politburo. Stalin appointed Kirov to replace Zinoviev as head of the Leningrad party organization. In 1930, after Kirov had backed Stalin's ouster of Bukharin, he was made a member of the Politburo. For the next three years he was a loyal Stalinist, continuing to follow the twists and turns of the dictator's policies as Stalin moved against the Trotskyites on the left and the followers of Bukharin on the right.

As the Leningrad party leader, Kirov was responsible for the Baltic–White Sea Canal Project, built between 1930 and May 1933. It had been constructed by slave laborers, former kulaks (or those accused of being kulaks, or sympathetic to kulaks). Built under "appalling conditions," workers' "deaths are reckoned at around 200,000" for the project.

Kirov received full and enthusiastic credit for the canal from Stalin. However, it was too narrow or too shallow for most ships, and "was in fact never of much use."[4]

DISSENT OR TREASON?

Negative feelings toward Stalin emerged at the Seventeenth Party Congress in February 1934. At that time "a number of delegates of the Congress . . . considered that the time had come to remove Stalin from the post of secretary general." The reason given was that he was "certain of his infallibility, he was beginning to ignore the principle of collective work, and was again becoming rude." Kirov, on the other hand, received a standing ovation from the congress when he rose to speak. Later, a group of delegates approached Kirov with the proposal that he replace Stalin.[5]

Kirov refused. He told Stalin of the offer, adding that "you yourself are to blame for what happened. After all, we told you things couldn't be done in such a drastic way."[6] This marked the beginning of a rift between them.

Meanwhile, Hitler and the Nazis had come to power in Germany. Stalin told the congress that this was no barrier to establishing friendly relations with Germany. Kirov disagreed. He also disagreed with Stalin about the harsh measures used to promote collectivization of farmlands. They exchanged sharp words over Kirov's insistence that Leningrad workers be supplied with more food. They quarreled over the brutality of the secret police.

Kirov believed he was just disagreeing with Stalin. It never occurred to him that he might be committing treason. That was a fatal miscalculation. The punishment for treason was death.

DESIGN FOR MURDER

"Many historians believe that Stalin himself ordered Kirov's murder."[7] They point to "evidence that Stalin had the secret police . . . arrange or allow the assassination of Kirov in order to eliminate a potential challenger."[8] Lord Alan Bullock writes that it was likely "that Stalin planned or at least authorized the murder."[9] Robert Conquest and fellow historian Dmitri Volkogonov agree.

The evidence is circumstantial but convincing. The assassin Nikolaev had twice before been arrested in proximity to Kirov while carrying a loaded gun. Both times he had been released "on orders from above" with no follow-up to the arrest.[10] The night of the murder, the usual guards on each floor of the Smolny Institute had been withdrawn. Kirov's bodyguard, Borisov, was detained outside by the secret police when Kirov entered the building. According to Nikita Khrushchev, in a speech to the Twenty-seventh Party Congress made after Stalin's death, when Borisov was summoned to the Smolny two days later to testify in the Nikolaev trial, he was murdered en route by secret police agents. They faked an accident, claiming that the truck they were in had "hit a warehouse wall," when Borisov "had in fact been killed by his guards with iron bars."[11] When Nikolaev was asked by Stalin himself why he had killed Kirov, the assassin pointed to the secret-police officers present and shouted that Stalin should ask them.

These secret-police agents were members of the People's Commissariat of Internal Affairs (NKVD). The NKVD was a reorganized version of the OGPU. The reorganization had taken place after the murder of OGPU head Vyacheslav Menzhinsky. He had been poisoned by a doctor acting for Genrich Yagoda, who would be appointed head of the NKVD by Stalin following Menzhinsky's death. Yagoda would later confess to his role in the murder of his predecessor.

At the time of Kirov's murder, Yagoda was "directly responsible to Stalin for all the operations of the Security Police." Yagoda would subsequently admit that he ordered his subordinates in the Leningrad NKVD "not to place any obstacles in the way of the terrorist act against Kirov." It was on Yagoda's authority that Nikolaev had been released after having been arrested with a gun, bullets, and a map of the route Kirov usually took to work.[12]

SPREADING THE TERROR

Immediately following Kirov's assassination, Stalin took two steps. He issued an emergency decree ordering a speedy investigation of "terrorist acts," and promptness in "carrying out death sentences."[13] He then personally took charge of the investigation into Kirov's murder.

Only three days after the assassination, arrests were announced of anti-Communist White Russians "charged with preparing terrorist attacks against workers of the Soviet power."[14] Between December 5 and December 18, 1934, 102 of the accused were tried, convicted, and executed. On December 21 it was announced that the Kirov assassination had been ordered by the "Leningrad opposition centre," a group of Zinoviev loyalists.[15] Nineteen people, including Zinoviev and Kamenev, were arrested and tried. The two former troika leaders admitted to having engaged in political activity that might have some responsibility for the Kirov murder, but no direct connection between them and Nikolaev was established. Nevertheless, Zinoviev was sentenced to ten years in prison, and Kamenev to five.

Mass arrests by the NKVD of those suspected of being associated with the Leningrad opposition center, or with Zinoviev, followed. The suspects were accused of being part of a vast conspiracy organized by the exiled Trotsky. The conspiracy was supposedly behind the Kirov assassination and also had planned to kill Stalin and other members of the Politburo. The object was allegedly to overthrow communism in Russia and reestablish capitalism.

Led by the NKVD, purges of those accused of disloyalty spread across the country. Party meetings were held in which members were urged to confess their deviations from the party line and to denounce colleagues guilty of disloyalty. Half a million members were expelled from the party, some merely for "failure to denounce" those who expressed doubts about Stalin's policies.[16] Dismissal from one's job usually followed expulsion from the party. Often, arrest followed expulsion.

Those expelled were shunned by friends and neighbors. The NKVD encouraged wives to divorce husbands who were arrested. They also urged children to turn in their parents. One thirteen-year-old girl was forced to tell a Communist youth organization meeting that she "approved of the shooting of her mother and father, as they were spies."[17]

STALIN'S PROMISE

In August 1936, a second round of trials began. Zinoviev and Kamenev were taken from prison and retried as coleaders of the Trotsky conspiracy.

Both were subjected to around-the-clock interrogation. Kamenev was told that his son would be shot if he didn't confess. Similar threats were made to Zinoviev.

Finally Stalin himself confronted Zinoviev and Kamenev and struck a deal with them. They would confess, no harm would come to their families, and they would not be executed. Stalin gave his word.

Zinoviev confessed on August 23. He confirmed the guilt of those on trial with him. He told the court that "through Trotskyism I arrived at Fascism." Kamenev also confessed, and then addressed his children. "Go forward," he told them. "Together with the Soviet people, follow Stalin."[18]

Two days later, NKVD executioners came for both men. Zinoviev became hysterical, screaming that Stalin had promised he would not be executed, and Stalin must keep his word. The NKVD officer pulled Zinoviev into the nearest cell and shot him there to shut him up.

THE TRIAL OF THE GENERALS

The terror continued. Sir John Lawrence of Keston College, formerly the Centre for the Study of Religion and Communism in Great Britain and former editor of an English-language newspaper in the USSR, estimates that "many hundreds of thousands" of Russian citizens "were shot." He writes that "no one was safe." Even "Communists were arrested on the suspicion that their very enthusiasm might lead them into forbidden paths. To hold a responsible post was to risk arrest, for any failure might be put down to sabotage." Lawrence observes that "the Jews suffered out of all proportion to their numbers, not because they were Jews but because most Jews had relations abroad." Foreign governments influenced by Jews like Trotsky were supposed to be behind the plot to bring down Stalin.[19]

NKVD trials of ordinary Russians were mostly held in secret. Trials of prominent figures like Zinoviev and Kamenev, however, were held in public. Foreign reporters and other observers were present at them. Often, impressed by the impassioned confessions of the accused, they became convinced that the guilty verdicts were just. Their reports influenced many in the United States and other countries that justice was being served in the USSR. However, as more trials followed those associated with the Kirov murder, more and more doubts were raised in other countries.

Nikolai Bukharin at a speech in December 1927, when he was the editor of the newspaper *Pravda*, which means truth.

In 1937, Nikolai Bukharin was arrested and held for thirteen months. Just before his arrest, when he was first accused of treason, the man who had helped Stalin oust Zinoviev and Kamenev protested the charges in the presence of the dictator. He read a statement declaring that there was a conspiracy "to set up an NKVD state and give Stalin unlimited power."[20] Six days later Bukharin was in prison.

During those six days, Stalin made a speech in which he portrayed the USSR as "encircled by hostile powers whose agents, recruited from Trotskyites with party cards and hiding behind Bolshevik masks, had penetrated all party, governmental, and economic organizations and were engaged in wrecking and espionage, not stopping short of murder."[21]

Stalin's first target was Yagoda, the head of the NKVD. Stalin blamed him for his organization's failure to rid the government of traitors and spies. Yagoda was fired, and the NKVD was purged of Yagoda loyalists. Some three thousand of them were executed in 1937. Yagoda himself was arrested and held for trial with Bukharin.

On June 11, 1937, nine members of the Red Army High Command were arrested and charged with conspiracy and treason. They were tried and executed the next day. Charges against other high-ranking military officers followed. According to Stalin, they were "puppets in the hands of the *Reichswehr* (German army)."[22] By the time it was over, 3 Soviet marshals, 13 army commanders, 8 admirals, 50 corps commanders, and 154 divisional commanders had been killed. In addition, 36,761 army officers and more than 3,000 naval officers had been dismissed. Stalin had wiped out the most experienced commanders in the USSR military.

THE BUKHARIN SHOW TRIAL

The public trial of Bukharin, Yagoda, and nineteen other defendants began in March 1938. The purpose of the prosecution was to link all elements of opposition to Stalin together as members of a giant conspiracy, which had been launched with the killing of Kirov. Among those accused, therefore, were members of the Politburo, the former head of the NKVD, the heads of government economic planning departments, leaders of four of the republics of the USSR, and diplomats who linked the others with both Trotsky and Germany.

All but one of those accused pleaded guilty. The pleas were accompanied by confessions that backed one another up. The confessions seemed heartfelt, sincere, and were extremely convincing. Once again, the foreign observers were impressed.

In some cases the NKVD had used physical torture to elicit admissions of guilt. However, "the basic NKVD method for obtaining confessions and breaking the accused man was the 'conveyor'—continual interrogation by relays of police for hours and days on end." When all else failed, the prisoner would be threatened with punishment against his family. Since 1935 a decree had been in effect that "extended full adult penalties down to children of twelve" for crimes committed by their parents.[23]

Once the prisoner had agreed to confess, there ensued a prolonged rehearsal period so that when he went on trial his confession would be convincing, and agree with and reinforce the confessions of others being tried with him. Yagoda admitted his role in the Kirov killing. Bukharin, on the other hand, while admitting the charges against him, told the court:"I categorically deny my complicity in the assassination of Kirov."[24]

All twenty-one defendants were convicted. On March 13, 1938, all except three were sentenced to death. Neither Yagoda nor Bukharin was among the three. Shortly before the sentence was carried out, Bukharin wrote a short note to Stalin. He addressed it to Koba, the alias Stalin had used in the old days when robbing banks to finance the revolution. "Koba," he asked, "why do you need me to die?"[25]

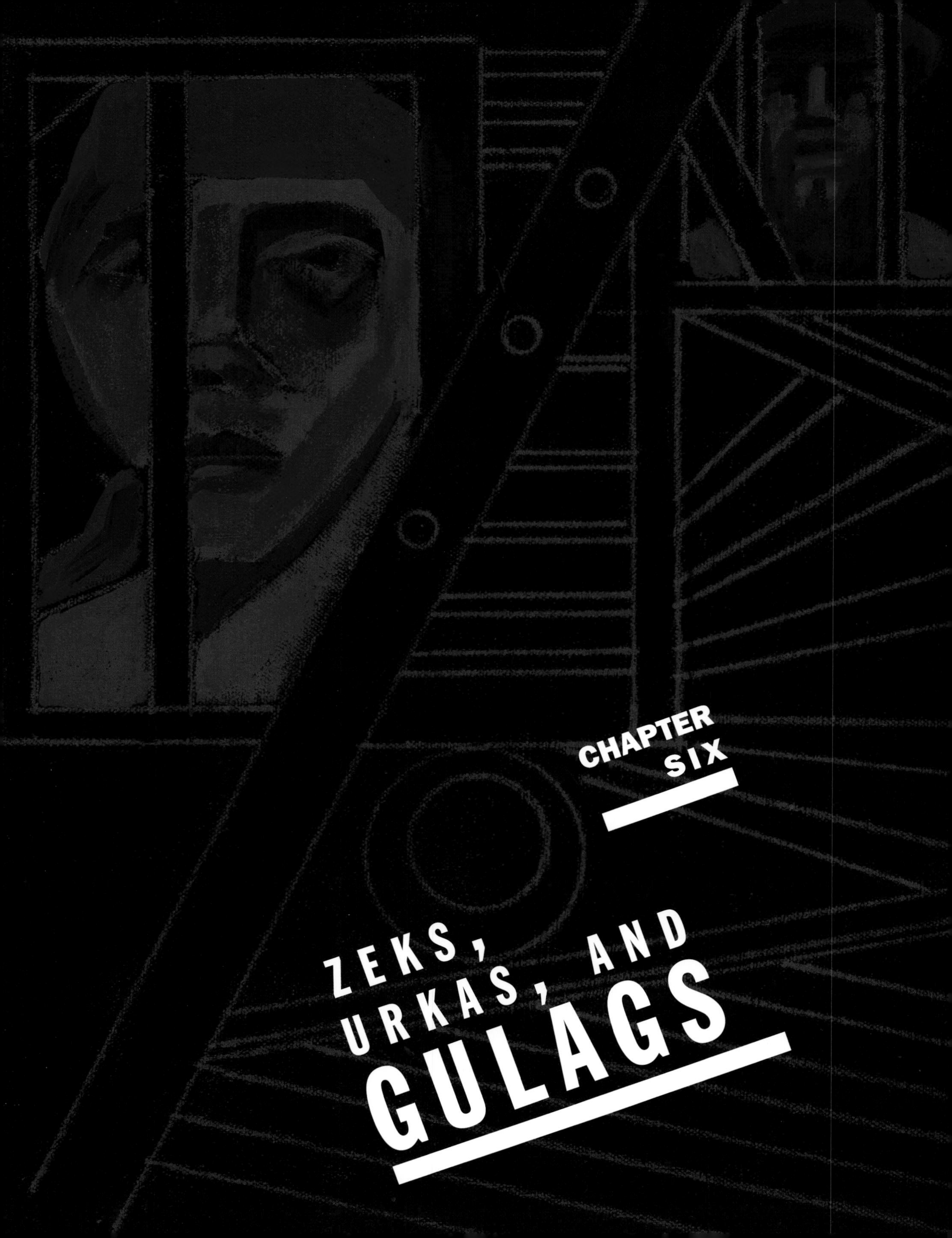

CHAPTER SIX

ZEKS, URKAS, AND GULAGS

Labour is a matter of honour, courage and heroism.

Inscription over the gates of Soviet gulag work camps

In June 1936, less than two years before he was executed for treason, Nikolai Bukharin completed work on a new Soviet constitution. Approved by both Stalin and the Politburo, the constitution became law in November. It guaranteed that people could not be arrested arbitrarily, that the privacy of their homes and of their correspondence would not be violated, that there would be freedom of speech and of the press, and that they could hold meetings and demonstrations. It instituted universal suffrage and direct elections of a Supreme Soviet composed of two legislative bodies similar in design to the U.S. Senate and House of Representatives. To Bukharin, it was "a document which would make it impossible for the people any longer to be 'pushed aside.'"[1]

He was wrong. The Communist party controlled all nominations to the Supreme Soviet, and Stalin, through the NKVD, controlled the Communist party. Nothing really changed. While many in the outside world applauded democratic reforms in the USSR, the purges continued.

TOEING THE PARTY LINE

World opinion was too often shaped by whatever information the Stalin regime chose to release. This was also true inside the USSR. Literature—

novels, nonfiction, plays—and media—newspapers, magazines, radio broadcasts—were all subject to strict government oversight. Much of this was accomplished through the Union of Soviet Writers, to which all writers had to belong in order to be published. The union monitored works by its members to be sure they conformed to Communist standards. Maxim Gorky, Isaak Babel, Boris Pasternak, and other acclaimed Russian writers had to submit to this oversight. Stalin personally checked on many of their books to be sure that they reflected positively on the Soviet Union. So it was that in the 1930s there were no novels or plays produced in the USSR that portrayed purges, famine, or suppression of opposition to collectivization. If such subjects were covered, it had to be done in such a way as to reflect glory on the policies of Stalin.

Scholars who published were likewise limited to the party line. In the field of economics, only pro-Marxist texts were permitted. Works by philosophers could not cast doubt on the theories of Marx and Engels. Any writings that might be considered Trotskyist were cause for arrest. Books on biology had to agree with the theories of Trofim Denisovich Lysenko, a favorite of Stalin whose theories of genetics and heredity had already been disproved. Even technical works on chemistry, physics, and engineering had to follow an approved party line.

Only volumes of history revised according to government standards were acceptable. Stalin commanded historians "to put the study of party history on to a scientific Bolshevik basis and to sharpen vigilance against Trotskyist and all other falsifiers of the history of our party."[2] Restrictions went well beyond Communist party history. Historians could be punished for anti-Marxist interpretations of non-Russian history as well. One historian was dismissed from his university post for not treating Joan of Arc as the Popular Front heroine of a national resistance movement. In general, historians were fair game for arrest by the NKVD. In 1937 there was actually a trial of a so-called terrorist group "consisting of historians" who had deviated from the Communist interpretation of the past.[3]

Other professors and teachers in universities were under constant surveillance. Thirteen secretaries of the Kiev Academy of Science were arrested, as were seven principals of Kiev University. Stalin's view of intellectuals as potential counterrevolutionaries resulted in the arrests of countless students as well as teachers. Renowned physicist Alexander Weissberg of the Kharkov Physics Institute, who was himself arrested, lamented the effect of arrests on training programs for physicists and engineers. "You need five years to train an engineer," he pointed out, "and even then the government had a very great deal of trouble before it could get suitable engineers for its new factories. But a capable physicist needs from ten to fifteen years training."[4]

PROPAGANDA AND REALITY

According to revelations made at the Twentieth Party Congress in 1956, "more than 600 writers who were guilty of no crime" were sentenced to prisons or work camps during the 1930s. Other writers, eager to prove their loyalty to communism and Stalin, produced Soviet propaganda in the guise of novels, short stories, and plays. Playwright Nikolai Pogodin was one of these. His drama, *The Aristocrats*, presented slave laborers as being both reformed and redeemed through the nobility of physical work. An old mother who visits her prisoner son finds joy in his physical development and healthy appearance. A prisoner is grateful for the lessons his imprisonment has taught him. "How beautifully you have re-educated me," he thanks his jailers. Another prisoner belts out his gratitude: "I am reborn, I want to live and sing," he carols.[5]

The truth of the Soviet work camps was very different. They were run by the Chief Administration of Corrective Labor Camps under the NKVD. The initials for this department in Russian were G-U-L-A-G. For that reason, the camps themselves became known as gulags. There was little or no gratitude toward jailers, or joyful singing, in the gulags.

There were three types of gulags. The first were defined as "factory and agricultural colonies where 'people deprived of freedom' are trained and disciplined." The second were "camps for mass works which includes those in 'distant regions' for 'class-dangerous elements' requiring 'a more severe regime." The third were "punitive camps for the 'strict isolation' of those 'previously detained in other colonies and showing persistent insubordination.'"[6]

In 1937 there were 35 groups of camps in as many regions. Each group contained approximately 200 camps. Each camp housed roughly 1,200 inmates. Because conditions were harsh, food rations scanty, and medical facilities short of supplies and personnel, the death rates in the camps were high. As a result, the turnover in the inmate population was rapid.

MASS EXECUTIONS

Although intellectuals were targeted, it was not the urban writers and scientists and university professors who made up the majority of the gulag prisoners, but rather the alleged kulaks from the vast farming areas of the USSR. They were looked down on as illiterate peasants by their jailers, and usually received much worse treatment than the intellectuals, who, regardless of being prisoners, still claimed a measure of respect from the NKVD. In the topsy-turvy world of Soviet politics, today's prominent urban prisoner might well be pardoned to become tomorrow's departmental bureaucrat. On the other hand, the personnel who ran the gulags made no distinction between genuine kulaks and the unfortunate illiterate peasants labeled as kulaks because of what were often illogical judgments.

The majority of these peasants were being punished for their resistance to the harsh enforcement by the NKVD of Stalin's policy of collectivization. "A significant element" in this resistance had been "the slaughter and consumption of livestock rather than surrendering it to the collective; in consequence, over half the national livestock resources were lost."[7] This had contributed to the food shortages, which plagued the USSR, and Stalin had ordered that those responsible be punished. Many peasants and their families were shot. Many more were sent to the gulags.

Being sentenced to the gulags was no guarantee of avoiding execution. There were periodic "orders from Moscow for the mass execution" of prisoners. There were no reasons given for such orders. According to records researched by author Lord Bullock, "some 50,000 prisoners are reported to have been transferred for execution . . . in the two years 1937 and 1938. They were tied up with wire like logs, stacked in trucks, driven outside the camp, and shot."[8]

Many prisoners never reached the gulags alive. They "did not survive the horrors of the railway journey which might last months, in overcrowded trucks, unheated in winter, unbearably hot in summer with inadequate food, water, and sanitation."[9] The NKVD train guards "were particularly brutal and negligent."[10] One survivor of the journey to the gulags reported that "there were whole days of twenty-four hours when not a drop of anything to drink passed into the cars. There were periods even of thirty-six hours."[11] The train trip from Leningrad to the camps at Vladivostok took forty-seven days.

SLAVE LABOR

Robbery of prisoners was common on the transports to the camps. Warm clothing, good shoes or boots, and any valuables might be taken by stealth or by force. The thieves might be NKVD guards, or they might be fellow prisoners who were criminals. About 10 to 15 percent of the prisoners were professional criminals. Many of them had grown up as orphans, children of parents who had died from famine or disease or had been murdered during the civil war or were among the purge victims. By an early age, these orphans were hardened hoodlums, better suited than most to survive in the gulags and had grouped together in juvenile gangs. They were known as *urkas*, and in the camps they often set up cruel governments of their own with rules and schedules for tributes to be paid. Just as often, they worked together with the camp authorities to maintain discipline among the other inmates who were looked down on as political prisoners.

The *urkas* often were exempt from the hardest jobs. All the other prisoners were slave laborers known as *zeks*. Some were peasants assigned to farms where, under NKVD supervision, they worked twice as hard as when they had tilled their own land. Sixteen-hour workdays were the rule. Nevertheless, they were the lucky ones. *Zeks* sent to the deep pits of coal, copper, and gold mines often were forced to work until they dropped. The turnover in the mines was frequent, and it was said that a healthy and athletic twenty year old could be turned into a skeleton in thirty to sixty days. This was not surprising since the basic food ration was around 800 grams (about 28 ounces) a day while the disciplinary ration—for those who had broken one of the many rules—was 300 grams (10.5 ounces). Those who worked in the lumber camps or at building new railway lines were slightly

Prisoners in this gulag near Archangel were forced to harvest, cut, and haul lumber. Prisoners of other gulags helped build roads, railroads, canals, and hydroelectric plants, as well as mine coal, copper, and gold.

better off, but not much. The railroad workers in Siberia, in particular, were subject to frostbite, and frequently lost fingers or toes.

In the early days, the first assignment of the prisoners was to build their own camps. In 1936, 600 prisoners were dumped in a forest in the area north of Archangel. They were assigned to build their own barracks, the first of a number of camps that would eventually house about 30,000 prisoners. They had only basic tools, and no horses to pull the sleds carrying the logs they had sawed from the trees they chopped down. The sleds were pulled—often for many miles—by teams of prisoners who were harnessed to them like mules to a plow. The teams were made up of either five men or seven women. These teams of women were among those later used to haul rails for construction of new railways.

WOMEN OF THE CAMPS

Among women prisoners in the gulags, there was a much higher percentage of criminals than among men. They looked down on the female political prisoners, and they bullied them. The only exceptions were nuns and other women imprisoned because of their connection with religion. These the female *urkas* treated with a respect they denied the peasants, all of whom they considered to be exploitative kulaks, and the intellectuals, whom they regarded as snobbish urban wimps.

Male *urkas* also treated these women badly. Author Robert Conquest reports that "non-criminal women were frequently mass-raped by *urkas*."[12] Sometimes women had sex with camp commandants in exchange for protection from the *urkas*. If the women refused to submit, they might be given the most brutal work tasks until they either gave in or dropped from the punishing labor. Sometimes they had sex with guards to obtain enough food to stay alive.

Like the men, women prisoners might be beaten for no reason. The majority of the camps were in Siberia, and if the women's shoes had been stolen, or had simply worn out, they might be forced to work barefoot in the bitter cold. One teenage girl, serving five years for stealing vegetables during the famine, tried to get out of work by crawling under the floorboards of her barracks. She was almost torn to pieces by the guard dogs who sniffed her out.

Nobody knows the exact number of women and men who spent time in Stalin's gulags in the late 1930s. According to historian Geoffrey Hosking, "estimates range from 3 million to 15 million."[13] Robert Conquest believes there were about eight million prisoners in the camps in 1938. Lord Bullock estimates that "between 1935 and 1937, their total population" was "six million men and women."[14] Whatever the correct number, many of these millions died. The purges that led to the gulags were a human tragedy of truly shocking dimensions.

Why did such a tragedy happen? Some believe that it was the inevitable result of a totalitarian and bureaucratic system such as communism. Others think that the NKVD, which controlled the gulags as well as the apparatus which sent people to them, simply got out of hand and ran amok. Many experts who have studied the period, however, see it as evidence of "a psychotic state of paranoid suspicion on the part of Stalin himself."[15] In other words, they believe that Stalin may simply have been a madman who used his absolute power to send vast numbers of people to the gulags, and millions to their death.

CHAPTER SEVEN

STRANGE BEDFELLOWS

> **Let every eye negotiate for itself**
> **And trust no agent.**
>
> William Shakespeare, *Much Ado About Nothing* (Act II, Sc. I)

On November 25, 1936, Germany and Japan signed the Anti-Comintern Pact, an agreement to collaborate in opposition to the Communist International, the organization sponsored by the Soviet Union to spread communism in other countries. Less than a year later, on November 6, 1937, Italy signed the pact.

STALIN'S PROBLEM

The published version of the Anti-Comintern Pact targeted communism with no mention of the USSR. However, a secret attachment pledged Germany and Japan to consult on action "to safeguard their common interests" in the event of conflict with the Soviet Union by either country. They agreed to "take no measures which would ease the situation of the Soviet Union." Translated from diplomatic language, that meant that in case of war, regardless of who provoked it, they would come to each other's aid against the USSR.[1]

Although the section about the Soviet Union was secret, Stalin well understood the danger of such an alliance. Both Germany and Japan were traditional enemies of Russia. The prospect of their simultaneously waging war against the USSR—Germany from the west, Japan from the east—alarmed Stalin.

In April 1935, the Soviet Union had signed an agreement of mutual assistance with France. Not long after the Anti-Comintern Pact was made public, in May 1937, Stalin sent an emissary to Paris to coordinate military activity between France and the USSR in case of war with Germany. The meeting failed when the French realized that "almost the entire command structure of the Red Army had been destroyed on Stalin's orders."[2]

Stalin was well aware of the problem he had created. His second Five-Year Plan, inaugurated in 1933, had concentrated on producing arms and weapons for the military. As a result, "Russia's defense industries expanded two and a half times as rapidly as Russian industry as a whole."[3] By 1937, Stalin was allocating 16.5 percent of the national budget to the rebuilding of the military. Over the next three years, he would raise that to more than 32.5 percent. However, he could not replace the officers he had exterminated. Instead, he installed a new young breed of Communist officers schooled in blind obedience both for themselves and for those they commanded. Rather than patriotism, pride, or camaraderie, the new Soviet army would be inspired by fear.

HITLER'S FORKED TONGUE

In the 1930s the leaders of the major nations in Europe, including Stalin, were playing a dangerous game. Hitler's Germany was on the march, and Europe was teetering on the brink of war. Many understandings had been reached and alliances formed between nations in anticipation of it.[4] When the Soviet Union had signed the mutual assistance agreement with France in 1935, it had also signed a similar pact with Czechoslovakia. A year earlier, Germany had signed a nonaggression pact with Poland. Great Britain and France had pledged to both Czechoslovakia and Poland that they would come to their aid if they were attacked. Hitler had given assurances that Nazi Germany had no designs on its neighbors.

Privately, to the leaders of his military forces, on November 5, 1937, Hitler had laid out a policy for acquiring additional territory for the German people. They had, he said, "the right to a greater living space than other peoples. . . . Germany's future was therefore wholly conditional upon the solving of the need for space."[5] He went on to proclaim the advantages of the "annexation of Czechoslovakia and Austria."[6] He shrugged off any intervention by the Soviet Union because he believed the purges had left their armed forces leaderless and too weak to risk conflict.

The USSR, however, was the ultimate target. "Everything I undertake is directed against the Russians," Hitler admitted. "If the West is too stupid and blind to grasp this, then I shall be compelled to come to an agreement with the Russians, beat the West, and then after their defeat turn against the Soviet Union with all my forces."[7]

BOTH SIDES OF THE STREET

Pacts and treaties, understandings and assurances, lost their meaning as secret—so-called back-channel—meetings were held between representatives of countries supposedly hostile to one another. Allies often were not informed of such contacts and negotiations. As Lord Bullock writes: "All the powers played on both sides of the street."[8]

As early as 1936, Stalin, supposedly the archenemy of Nazism, "began to put out feelers to the Nazis" regarding "the possibility of enlarging Soviet-German trade."[9] In January 1937, Hitler rejected the Russian overtures, but told his diplomats that the door should be kept open to future negotiations depending on events inside the Soviet Union. He thought that the purges going on at that time indicated that Stalin was moving to the political right.

A year later, in March 1938, Hitler's good-neighbor promises proved meaningless as Nazi troops marched into Austria. The annexation of Austria by Germany, known as *anschluss,* was voted on by the populations of both countries on April 10. Ninety-nine percent of the voters in both nations approved the takeover.

PRESSURING CZECHOSLOVAKIA

Next Hitler turned toward Czechoslovakia. His excuse for the *anschluss* had been the large number of German-speaking citizens with German blood living in Austria. Now he cited the large number of Germans living and working in the Sudetenland region of Czechoslovakia as the excuse for annexing that area to Germany. Nazi propaganda had stirred up Germans in the Sudetenland to agitate for such a move.

Events moved quickly. The Soviet Union, Great Britain, and France had all signed pledges to come to Czechoslovakia's aid in case of attack. In May 1938, to defend themselves against an expected invasion, the Czechs placed 400,000 troops on their border with Germany. Throughout the spring and summer of 1938, Moscow repeatedly assured the Czechs that "the USSR was able and willing to defend Czechoslovakia from impending invasion."[10] However, in July the British government asked the Czechs "to make concessions to Sudetens to appease Nazis."[11]

When the Czechs refused, the Nazis called up one million reserves to beef up the German military forces. On August 15 the German army began war maneuvers near the Czech border. Great Britain reversed itself and responded by warning Germany that an attack on the Czechs would mean a new world war. However, Great Britain, and France as well, were not prepared to back up that threat. Their timidity led to a historic meeting in Munich on September 29, 1938.

"PEACE IN OUR TIME"

The four-power Munich Conference was attended by Prime Minister Neville Chamberlain of Great Britain, Premier Édouard Daladier of France, Premier Benito Mussolini of Italy, and the führer of Germany and Austria, Adolf Hitler. The sole topic was the Czechoslovakian crisis, but no representative of Czechoslovakia was present. The Soviet Union was not invited to attend, probably because of the participants' strong anti-Communist policies. The meeting resulted in the transfer of the Sudetenland, from Czechoslovakia to Germany. In return, Hitler gave guarantees that there would be no aggression against the rest of Czechoslovakia. France and Great Britain went along with this. Prime Minister Chamberlain announced that it would mean "peace in our time."[12]

Stalin was furious at being left out of the negotiations. He considered it an insult to the Soviet Union on the part of Great Britain and France. He decided that if they would not defend Czechoslovakia, then his country had no obligation to act alone. He also feared that the agreement by the four powers involved might signal that Britain and France, capitalist nations with no fondness for communism, might join Germany, Italy, and Japan in the Anti-Comintern Pact.

On March 10, 1939, in a speech to the Eighteenth Communist Party Congress in Moscow, Stalin made his reaction to Munich clear. He said that France and Great Britain had "abandoned the principle of collective security" in order to "divert the aggressor States to other victims." He accused them of "pushing the Germans farther eastward, promising them an easy prey and saying: 'Just start a war with the Bolsheviks, everything else will take care of itself.'" However, he pledged "not to let our country be drawn into conflict by warmongers, whose custom it is to let others pull their chestnuts out of the fire."[13]

As if to prove Stalin right, five days later, on March 15, 1939, the pledge Hitler made at Munich was broken as Nazi troops began the occupation of the rest of Czechoslovakia. Again, France, Britain, and the Soviet Union did not act. However, on April 1, Prime Minister Chamberlain issued a statement that if Germany attacked Poland, Britain and France would declare war. Hitler's response strangely echoed Stalin's words. He said, "Whoever declares himself ready to pull the chestnuts out of the fire of the big powers, must expect to burn his fingers in the attempt."[14]

LET'S MAKE A DEAL

Throughout the spring and summer of 1939, the major European powers jockeyed to realign their alliances. In the face of Stalin's suspicions about their motives at Munich, Britain and France stepped up "efforts for an agreement with the Soviet Union."[15] Meanwhile, there were ongoing contacts between the Soviets and the Germans, who were trying to "build bridges" between their two countries.[16] At the same time, "secret Anglo-German talks were also going on in London."[17] However, the main focus was Moscow, "with the British and French competing with the Germans for Stalin's favor."[18]

Neville Chamberlain of Great Britain, Édouard Daladier of France, Adolf Hitler of Germany, and Benito Mussolini of Italy (left to right) met in Munich in 1938 to form an agreement about Czechoslovakia.

By this time trade talks between the Russians and Germans were proceeding. These were important to Stalin because trade with Germany would mean a big boost to the Soviet economy. For Germany it meant having access to Russian resources such as surplus wheat to feed its people, and oil and steel to beef up its military machine. On August 15, a note was passed on to Stalin from the German government stating that "there is no question which cannot be settled to the complete satisfaction of both countries."[19] It went on to specifically include Poland as an area on which there could be agreement. Stalin replied that before this could be discussed a trade accord must be reached.

The trade pact was quickly finalized and signed by both sides. Then, on August 19, the Germans informed the Russians that "there is fear in Berlin of a conflict between Germany and Poland." This was followed by a letter from Hitler to Stalin the next day pressing for a nonaggression pact between their two countries because "the tension between Germany and Poland has become insupportable."[20] On August 23, Nazis and Communists "signed a non-aggression treaty that stymied efforts in Paris and London to restrain Adolph Hitler."[21] It was called a nonaggression pact, but it was much more than that. It was an agreement to coordinate military efforts in the invasion and occupation of Poland.

German troops crossed the border into Poland on September 1, 1939. Living up to their pledge to defend Poland, France and Great Britain declared war on Germany. On September 17, Soviet troops pushed into Poland from the east. A joint German-Russian communiqué said their troops would "bring order to Poland." In the division of Poland that followed, the Soviet Union gained control of "76,500 square miles [198,135 square km] of the eastern region of the nation with its population of 12.8 million" people.[22]

World War II had begun. France and Britain, facing Hitler's superior war machine, did not declare war on the Soviet Union. For the present, Stalin could enjoy his seizure of Polish territory and contemplate future conquests. With his ally Hitler fighting the British and French, he didn't have to fear his capitalist foes in the West. But then again, with a friend like Hitler, who needed enemies?

CHAPTER EIGHT

TRIUMPH AND TREACHERY

I know how much the German people loves its Führer. I should therefore like to drink his health.

Joseph Stalin, celebrating the 1939 nonaggression treaty between the Soviet Union and Germany

As World War II broke out in Europe, other countries were struggling to make sense of the alliance between two countries locked into such opposing philosophies as communism and Nazism. The leaders of Japan, the first nation to sign the Anti-Comintern Pact with Nazi Germany, were furious at Hitler's betrayal. In the United States, the reaction to the Hitler-Stalin pact and the brutal invasion of Poland, which followed, was one of shocked disbelief.

The Great Depression was not yet over in 1939, and while membership in the American Communist party was low, support for it among humanists and liberals had been at its peak before the Soviet Union allied itself with Germany. The party was a legal organization under United States law, and it was legal to be a member of it. Nevertheless, some Americans regarded it with suspicion. As early as 1937, the Comintern had "announced it intended to infiltrate American labor unions." The U.S. State Department had reacted with a "most emphatic protest," claiming the move interfered with "the maintenance of friendly relations" between the Soviet Union and the United States.[1]

AN AMERICAN WAKE-UP CALL

As 1938 began, the census recorded nearly eight million jobless people in the United States. While this was half the number of jobless people at the start of the depression, it nevertheless meant that a fifth of the American workforce was still unemployed. African Americans were the worst off. The American Communist party supported their causes, propagandized them, and targeted them for membership. Those people who supported equal rights and work programs for African Americans, as well as a host of other causes, were labeled dupes or fellow travelers by anti-Communists.

Pressure from these anti-Communists had resulted in Congress forming a committee to investigate the link between the Soviet Comintern and the American Communist party. The head of the party, Earl Browder, was called to testify. He admitted to a connection between Moscow and the party. He added that the party was not opposed to the present New Deal government of Franklin D. Roosevelt, and that it supported "any or all institutions of American democracy whereby the American people have obtained power to determine their own destiny to any degree."[2]

Browder's statement assured liberals that the party and the New Deal were on the same track. It also reinforced the suspicion of anti-Communists that the New Deal itself was staffed by Communist fellow travelers. At this point, pro-Nazi Americans were strongly anti-Communist. Some of them had other agendas. One, Father Charles Coughlin, a priest who had been censured by the Vatican, told a radio audience on November 27, 1938, that "the Russian Revolution of 1917 was financed by Jewish groups."[3] His anti-Semitic views, like his speeches attacking President Franklin Roosevelt, reflected the policies of the Nazi Bund and other pro-Hitler American groups.

These groups were stunned by the Hitler-Stalin pact. So, too, were those, who had supported the Communist party. Many of those who had joined the party left. Many who had allied themselves with it in various causes now backed away in horror. It had been a matter of principle to support a group that was prolabor and antidiscrimination. It was unthinkable to go along with a Nazi ally.

THE FOURTH INTERNATIONAL

One American who had jumped neither on the pro-Communist nor anti-Communist bandwagon was the renowned philosopher and educator John Dewey. In 1933, he had been one of the founders of the University-in-Exile, "established for scholars being persecuted in countries under totalitarian regimes." Four years later this led him to Mexico City as head of a commission of inquiry "to hear Leon Trotsky's rebuttal of the charges made against him in the Moscow trials of 1936 and 1937."[4] Trotsky had been accused in the purge trials of conspiring with Germany and Japan to form "an anti-Soviet alliance."[5] Testifying before the Dewey Commission, Trotsky convincingly denied the charges while at the same time calling for the overthrow of Stalin. Trotsky was convinced that the charges against him would turn out to be true of Stalin himself.

Trotsky still had contacts within the Soviet government. By 1938 he was aware that secret trade negotiations were going on with Germany. He realized that the Comintern—the Third International—was supporting those negotiations by withholding support from the anti-Nazi German Communist party. This led Trotsky to Perigny, France, where on September 3, 1938, he headed a conference to establish the Fourth International in opposition to the Comintern. The Fourth International declared an anti-Stalinist policy and a Transitional Program, which called for immediate goals of "higher wages and better working conditions" with the eventual objective of "the overthrow of capitalism and the transition to Socialism." The United States branch called itself the "Socialist Workers party (SWP)."[6]

The Fourth International organized "anti-Stalinist splinter groups from numerous Communist parties around the world."[7] In effect, it "placed Stalin on the same level as Hitler, which Stalin found intolerable."[8] To Stalin, signing a pact with the Nazi devil was in no way the same thing as *being* the devil.

MURDER MOST FOUL

As war broke out in September 1939, Stalin had more pressing concerns than Trotsky. Nevertheless, he could not simply dismiss Trotsky from his mind, so he took steps to have him eliminated.

On May 24, 1940, the bedroom of Trotsky's home in Coyoacán, Mexico, was sprayed with bullets. The gunmen were disguised in the uniforms of the local police. Trotsky and his wife shielded themselves behind some furniture and emerged unhurt. When the genuine Mexican police asked Trotsky if he had any idea who was responsible, he replied that "the author of the attack is Iosif [Joseph] Stalin."[9]

Three months later violence struck again. A visitor well known to Trotsky brought him the manuscript of an unpublished article for his comments. Known to Trotsky as a Canadian named Jacson, his real name was Ramon del Rio Mercader, and he was a Spaniard working for Stalin. As Trotsky pored over the manuscript, Mercader took an ice pick out of his raincoat. He closed his eyes and plunged it into Trotsky's head with full force. Trotsky, according to testimony by Mercader, "gave a terrible piercing cry."[10]

However, Trotsky was not yet dead. He was rushed to a hospital in Mexico City. There he clung to life for twenty-four hours. At the very end, in a whisper, he declared that "I am sure of the victory of the Fourth International."[11]

COMMUNIZING POLAND

Trotsky's death was the climax of a busy time for Stalin. The vast territory of Poland that the USSR took over at the beginning of World War II had to be reorganized. The troops that occupied it had to set up local Communist governments to rule it. Polish institutions had to be restructured along strict Communist lines. This meant abolishing private property, nationalizing industry and businesses, collectivizing farms, and creating local workers' soviets under a Polish Communist party. A Communist-controlled election resulted in an assembly whose delegates voted for eastern Poland to be split up and annexed by the Ukrainian Soviet Socialist Republic and the Byelorussian Soviet Socialist Republic. Supervision from Moscow—which meant Stalin—was imposed every step of the way.

Russian Communist political officers provoked "the poorer peasants to attack Polish landlords, kulaks and policemen, revenging themselves for the wrongs they had suffered and the grudges they had accumulated."

German troops parade in front of Hitler and other Nazi generals on October 5, 1939, after Germany's invasion of Poland.

Those who fell victim to such mobs often were tortured before they were killed. Old prejudices were revived and released. Pogroms—riots and killing sprees—against Jews were frequent. The occupying Red Army shrugged them off as "the inevitable accompaniment of the 'revolution'" they supported.[12]

In western Poland, the conquering German army was followed by Nazi mop-up forces assigned to massacre Jews. It was the beginning of the Holocaust, which eventually would take six million Jewish lives. Many Jews fled east—to Soviet-conquered Poland and to the interior regions of the USSR. Hundreds of thousands of Polish Jews saved their lives in this way. Some, however, encountered traditional Polish, Ukrainian, and Russian anti-Semitism and were killed.

The NKVD had moved into eastern Poland as soon as the Red Army secured the area. It carried out a program similar to the purges in Soviet Russia. Actions were aimed at the former ruling class, Polish intellectuals (teachers, professors, philosophers, writers), preinvasion government officials, clergy, judges, and others who were not peasants. One victim who managed to survive described it as "beheading the community."[13] Torture, imprisonment, and execution took a heavy toll.

THE WINTER WAR

Stalin's plan in occupying eastern Poland was to militarize it as "the centerpiece of a broad defensive belt of territory against invasion from the west." He struck a deal with Hitler, which gave the Nazis the districts of Poland containing the major cities of Warsaw and Lubin in exchange for the Soviets taking over much of the territory of the nation of Lithuania. Prior to World War I, Lithuania had been part of tsarist Russia. So, too, had the other two Baltic nations—Latvia and Estonia—as well as Finland. Now Stalin wanted these territories back, and with Hitler occupied in the west with his war against Britain and France, Stalin "forced treaties on the three Baltic states allowing the Soviet Union to garrison bases on their territory." Subsequently the Red Army seized control of the three nations, installed so-called popular governments, and in effect took them over.[14]

Finland was another matter, and one which greatly frustrated Stalin. Back in 1917, Stalin had represented the Bolshevik government when it granted Finland its independence from Russia. Now, in 1939, he was demanding that Finland turn over certain strategic territory to the USSR. The Finns refused. Soviet troops and tanks crossed the Finnish border on November 30. It was the start of what would come to be known as the Winter War.

Marshal Kliment Y. Voroshilov, the Soviet commissar for defense, assured Stalin that Finland would fall in six days. However, Voroshilov had not reckoned with the bitterly cold Finnish winter. Russian troops were not equipped for it. They lacked the necessary arctic uniforms and winter gear. The white fur-wearing Finns skied circles around them in the blinding snow, sighting their weapons with the help of sunglasses, wreaking havoc, and vanishing into the whiteness of the landscape to retreat behind their heavily fortified Mannerheim Line. A Russian general summed up the humiliation of the Soviet Seventh Army: "We have conquered just enough Finnish territory to allow us to bury our dead," he sighed.[15]

A TAINTED VICTORY

The Soviet nation had lost face. To the people—and to Stalin himself—Stalin was the nation. That was the essence of the cult of personality which kept him in power. Now, however, the high casualties suffered by the Red Army raised questions about his judgment. The Winter War was increasingly unpopular. Stalin was forced to take strong action.

He mobilized the full resources of the Red Army for a massive attack against the Finns. It began on January 15, 1940, with a bombardment of the Mannerheim Line. Heavy shelling went on without pause for sixteen days. Then a thousand tanks moved on the Finns, followed by 140,000 crack Soviet troops. Despite the strength of the attack, the greatly outnumbered Finns held them off for more than two weeks. Finally, on February 22, the Finns retreated to new positions.

Stalin's worries, however, were not yet over. He was receiving reports that the British and French were planning to send supplies and troops to bolster the Finnish resistance. What had begun as a local action to regain

Finnish soldiers during the Winter War of 1939–1940

territory, which had once been part of Russia, now threatened to become a general war with Britain and France. It was true that they were at war with Germany, but they had not declared war on Hitler's ally, the Soviet Union. Stalin wanted to avert such a war at all costs.

Following the Finnish retreat, Stalin made a peace offer. He again demanded that the Finns turn over strategic territories to the Soviet Union in return for allowing Finland to retain its independence. The Finns did not reply immediately. They, too, expected help from the British and French. However, the timing was against them. By the time Great Britain and France got around to notifying the Finns that they would send troops and planes to fight the Soviets, the Finnish army had exhausted its reserves, and the choice was between being overrun by the Reds and accepting Stalin's terms. On March 12, 1940, the Finns capitulated.

The Winter War was over. Stalin saw to it that Russian casualty figures were not made public. Finland's Marshal Carl Mannerheim estimated a total of 200,000 Soviet soldiers killed. It was not, however, the loss of men that troubled Stalin. It was the loss of prestige for himself, and more critically, for the Red Army, which would undoubtedly one day have to fight a much more major war.

THE PHONY WAR

Stalin may have been a tyrant, a murderer, and a madman, but he was not a fool. He recognized the fragility of the pact with Germany. He knew that Hitler had targeted the Soviet Union to destroy communism, to take over its vast lands for German expansion, and for its deposits of oil and iron ore. His mistake was that he thought Germany would bog down in the war with France and Britain, and that any attack on the USSR would occur far in the future. Stalin had "counted on the sort of stalemate that had developed in 1914—or at least on a campaign that would last a year or two, seriously weaken the Germans, even if they won, and leave him time to strengthen Russia's defenses."[16] He had not anticipated the Nazi blitzkrieg.

In German, blitzkrieg translates as "lightning war." Webster's dictionary defines it as a "swift, sudden, overwhelming attack."[17] Both definitions fit the onslaught of the German army in the summer of 1940.

For the six months prior to that, Stalin had reason to think his appraisal of Germany's war with France and Britain in Western Europe was correct. It was a period of very little actual fighting. Even when the collapse of Poland allowed the Germans to move several divisions to the west, where they faced forty-one divisions of the French army entrenched in the underground concrete structures of the fortresslike Maginot Line, there was very little action. As Stalin saw it, all was quiet on the western front for the Germans, and the journalists had reason to call it the "Phony War."[18]

BLITZKRIEG!

The Phony War was still going on when German troops attacked neutral Denmark on April 9, 1940. The real target was Norway, which controlled the North Sea passage used by the British, French, and German navies. Norway immediately declared war on Germany, but it was no use. Germany's air power and paratroopers prevailed, and Nazi forces quickly occupied both countries.

A month later, a German blitzkrieg circled the Maginot Line to invade Belgium and the Netherlands, two other countries that had been neutral. The surprise attacks began with the bombing of Dutch and Belgian airfields and the strafing of civilians. Four hundred Belgians were killed during a nightlong bombing of the Antwerp airport. Tanks crashed across both borders, and crack German divisions followed them to seize strategic military objectives. German paratroopers, "some dressed in Dutch military uniforms," dropped from the sky.[19] Four days later the Dutch surrendered. The Belgians followed suit on May 28.

Bypassing the Maginot Line and the French armies reinforcing it, the blitzkrieg continued into France to overwhelm the French Second and Ninth armies—infantry units with no antitank guns or antiaircraft artillery to back them up. The only significant troops in the way of the Germans now were those of the British Expeditionary Force. They fought a gallant holding action, but were pushed farther and farther back toward the coastline of France.

By May 26, the British were trapped with their backs to the sea, facing "imminent annihilation." Amazingly, "Hitler ordered a halt to the assault."[20]

This enabled the British to regroup at Dunkirk on the French coast. On June 4, in one of "Britain's greatest military achievements," the Royal Navy, aided by hundreds of small privately-owned vessels, successfully evacuated 340,000 troops from Dunkirk and brought them back safely to England. Disaster had been averted; Britain would live to fight another day.

OPERATION BARBAROSSA

Stalin was alarmed. Had Hitler halted the attack on the British to signal his willingness to make a separate peace in order to turn eastward to invade the Soviet Union? When German troops occupied Paris on June 14, and then France signed an armistice on June 22, Stalin's apprehension increased. However, he was no more consistent in his fears than he had always been in his politics. When, early in 1941, the Germans and Italians mounted a campaign against the British in North Africa, he convinced himself that there was no immediate danger. After all, the Germans also were occupied in Greece, where they had been forced to send reinforcements to keep an Italian invasion of that country from failing. At the same time, Nazi troops had overrun Yugoslavia. Surely the Germans were too busy to turn toward the Soviet Union just yet.

There was additional reassurance in the results of Stalin's negotiations with Japan. The fear always had been of a simultaneous attack by Germany from the west and Japan from the east. That threat was eliminated in April 1941, when the Soviet Union and Japan signed a Neutrality Pact. The Japanese never had gotten over their feelings of betrayal when Hitler forged an alliance with the Soviet Union. Now, like Germany, they too were resigning from the Anti-Comintern Pact.

Stalin did not know that as early as November 1940, Hitler and his general staff were planning "Operation Barbarossa, for the invasion of the USSR."[21] When, on June 12 and June 15, 1941, information was received that "the Germans might be about to attack, Moscow treated the warning with contempt."[22] Stalin believed that while "Russia could not escape an eventual war with Germany, it would not occur until 1942 or 1943, leaving him two to three years longer to prepare for it."[23]

That belief was shattered when Operation Barbarossa was launched on June 22, 1941. Two armies of 120 divisions stampeded across the Russian border at two points, sweeping aside Russian defenses and taking 300,000 prisoners in the first five days. Stalin was asleep when the attack began. Awakened at 3:30 A.M., he seemed "unwilling, or unable to grasp the situation." He argued that if it really was war, "there would surely have been a formal declaration." When it was confirmed that Hitler had indeed declared war on the USSR, "Stalin still found it difficult to take in what was happening."[24]

When he recovered, however, he would behave like his old self. During the four years of war that followed, Stalin would rule the country with an iron hand. Heedless of the value of human life, he would give the orders pushing his people into the jaws of death. Millions upon millions of Soviet citizens would lose their lives doing his bidding. In the war, as he had during the purges, Stalin would repeatedly demonstrate that "absolute power corrupts absolutely."[25]

CHRONOLOGY

1917—November 7—Bloodless Bolshevik revolution succeeds in seizing control of the government of Russia.
November 15—Declaration of the Rights of Peoples gives tsarist territories the option to set up independent states.
December—Cheka (Soviet Russian secret-police organization) is established.

1919—March 2—Third Communist International (Comintern) is created.

1920–21—Vladimir Lenin introduces New Economic Policy (NEP) giving peasants land ownership.

1922—Union of Soviet Socialist Republics (USSR) is established.
April—Joseph Stalin appointed general secretary of Russian Communist party.
May—Central Committee of Communist party passes over Leon Trotsky in favor of leadership troika of Grigori Zinoviev, Lev Kamenev, and Stalin. Lenin asks Trotsky to remove Stalin; Trotsky tries and fails, and is condemned by party for "anti-Marxist deviation."

1923—January—China's Kuomintang (KMT) agrees to let Comintern reorganize it along Communist lines.

1924—January 21—Vladimir Lenin dies; Stalin begins his brutal thirty-year dictatorship.

1925—March—Chiang Kai-shek begins purge of Communists from the Kuomintang.
December—Zinoviev and Kamenev challenge Stalin's policies at the Fourteenth Party Congress.
December—Trotsky, Zinoviev, and Kamenev are thrown out of the Communist party.

1928—January—Trotsky is arrested and exiled.
March—First show trials are held in Moscow.
May—Stalin proclaims collectivization of agriculture, in effect ending the NEP.
November—First Five-Year Plan begins; former militant Stalinist Nikolai Bukharin is removed from the Politburo.

1930—Comintern organizes Communist party of Indochina.
September—Indochinese Communists attack landlords in French colony of Vietnam.

1932—Franklin D. Roosevelt is elected president of depression-era United States.
November—Stalin's second wife commits suicide.
December—First Five-Year Plan meets goals in four years; second Five-Year Plan begins.

1933—November—United States recognizes USSR.
December—Comintern inaugurates Popular Front policy.

1934—February—Following attacks on Stalin at Seventeenth Party Congress, Sergei Kirov is approached to replace Stalin, but refuses.
December—Kirov is assassinated; 102 people convicted of involvement in Kirov's killing are executed.

1935—Purges and executions mount throughout the Soviet Union.

April—Stalin signs mutual assistance agreement with France and Czechoslovakia.

1936—Bukharin completes new Soviet constitution.
July—Spanish Civil War begins.
August—Zinoviev and Kamenev confess to involvement in a Trotskyist conspiracy and are executed.
November—Germany and Japan sign Anti-Comintern Pact.

1937—Comintern announces intention to infiltrate American labor unions.
Bukharin and former secret-police chief Genrich Yagoda are arrested and charged with treason.
April—German planes bomb Guernica, Spain, and strafe civilians.
June—Nine members of the Red Army High Command are executed; other top officers are killed or dismissed; the Soviet military is left virtually leaderless.
November—Italy signs Anti-Comintern Pact.

1938—March—After thirteen months of imprisonment, Bukharin and Yagoda are tried and executed; Germany annexes Austria.
September—Anti-Stalin Fourth International is formed by Trotsky; Munich meeting gives Czechoslovakia's Sudetenland to Hitler in exchange for "peace in our time."

1939—March—Nazi troops take over the rest of Czechoslovakia; Communists and anti-Communists battle in Madrid, enabling the Falange to capture the city; Spanish Civil War ends.
August—Soviet Union signs nonaggression pact with Nazi Germany.
September—First Germany and then the Soviet Union invade Poland.
November—The Winter War begins with Soviet invasion of Finland.

1940—USSR takes over Latvia, Lithuania, and Estonia; Nazis and allies occupy Denmark, Norway, the Netherlands, Belgium, Yugoslavia, and Greece; France is defeated; British forces are evacuated from Dunkirk.
March—The Winter War ends and Finland cedes strategic territory to Soviet Union. August—Trotsky is assassinated.

1941—Germany and Italy attack British in North Africa.
April—Soviet Union and Japan sign Neutrality Pact.
June 22—Operation Barbarossa, the Nazi invasion of the Soviet Union is launched.

CHAPTER ONE

1. Dmitri Volkogonov, *Stalin: Triumph & Tragedy* (New York: Grove Weidenfeld, 1991), p. xxiii.
2. Alan Bullock, *Hitler and Stalin: Parallel Lives* (New York: Alfred A. Knopf, 1992) p. 133.
3. Bullock, p. 133.
4. Richard Pipes, *Russia Under the Bolshevik Regime* (New York: Alfred A. Knopf, 1993), p. 487.
5. Pipes, p. 488.
6. *Encyclopaedia Britannica,* vol. 16 (Chicago: Encyclopaedia Britannica, 1984), p. 72.
7. *Encyclopaedia Britannica,* vol. 16, p. 72.
8. Volkogonov, p. 7.
9. Author uncredited. *Joseph Stalin* (NYPL Electronic Resources: Biography Resource Center, *Historic World Leaders,* Gale Research, 1994), p. 1.
10. Bullock, p. 27.
11. Volkogonov, p. 5.
12. Orlando Figes, *A People's Tragedy: A History of the Russian Revolution* (New York: Viking, 1997), p. 387.
13. Figes, p. 387.

14. Richard Pipes, *The Russian Revolution* (New York: Alfred A. Knopf, 1990), pp. 432–433.

CHAPTER TWO

1. Alan Bullock, *Hitler and Stalin: Parallel Lives* (New York: Alfred A. Knopf, 1992), p. 116.
2. William J. Miller, Henry L. Roberts, and Marshall D. Shulman, *The Meaning of Communism* (Morristown, NJ: Silver Burdett Company, 1963), pp. 79–80.
3. Author uncredited. *Leon Trotsky* (NYPL Electronic Resources: Biography Resource Center, *Encyclopedia of World Biography,* Gale Research, 1998), p. 3.
4. *Encyclopaedia Britannica,* vol. 16 (Chicago: Encyclopaedia Britannica, 1984), p. 73.
5. *Encyclopaedia Britannica,* vol. 16, p. 72.
6. Geoffrey Hosking, *The First Socialist Society: A History of the Soviet Union from Within* (Cambridge, MA: Harvard University Press, 1993), p. 120.
7. Brian Crozier, *The Rise and Fall of the Soviet Empire* (Rocklin, CA: Prima Publishing, 1999), p. 35.
8. Hosking, pp. 121–122.
9. Bullock, p.195.
10. Bullock, p.196.
11. Bullock, pp. 198–199.
12. Bullock, pp. 200–201.

CHAPTER THREE

1. Geoffrey Hosking, *The First Socialist Society: A History of the Soviet Union from Within* (Cambridge, MA: Harvard University Press, 1993), pp. 69–70.
2. Hosking, p. 140.
3. *Encyclopaedia Britannica,* vol. 7 (Chicago: Encyclopaedia Britannica, 1984), p. 494.
4. Alan Bullock, *Hitler and Stalin: Parallel Lives* (New York: Alfred A. Knopf, 1992), p. 210.
5. Bullock, p. 210.
6. *Encyclopaedia Britannica,* vol. 6, p. 256.

7. Dmitri Volkogonov, *Stalin: Triumph & Tragedy* (New York: Grove Weidenfeld, 1991), p. 181.
8. Volkogonov, pp. 181–183.
9. Bullock, p. 211.
10. Volkogonov, p. 183.
11. Bullock, p. 206-207
12. Bullock, p. 207.
13. Volkogonov, p. 165.
14. Bullock, p. 207.
15. Volkogonov, p. 166.
16. Winston Churchill, *History of the Second World War, vol. 4: The Hinge of Fate* (London: Cassell Reference, 1951), pp. 447–448.
17. *Chronicle of the 20th Century* (Mount Kisco, NY: Chronicle Publications, 1987), p. 390.
18. Bullock, p. 374.

CHAPTER FOUR

1. Brian Crozier, *The Rise and Fall of the Soviet Empire* (Rocklin, CA: Prima Publishing, 1999), p. 44.
2. *Encyclopaedia Britannica,* vol. 5 (Chicago: Encyclopaedia Britannica, 1984), p. 384.
3. Author uncredited. *Chiang Kai-shek* (NYPL Electronic Resources: Biography Resource Center, *Encyclopedia of World Biography,* Gale Research, 1998), p. 2.
4. *Chiang Kai-shek*, p. 2.
5. Crozier, p. 46.
6. Crozier, p. 47.
7. *Chiang Kai-shek*, p. 2.
8. *Chiang Kai-shek*, p. 3.
9. Crozier, p. 51.
10. Crozier, p. 53.
11. Francesca Patai, *"La Pasionaria"—Dolores Ibarurri (1895–1989)* from *People's Weekly World,* March 15, 1997, Internet: <www.cpusa.org/cp-usa/archives97/97-03-15-3.html>, pp. 1, 3.
12. Patai, p. 1.
13. Patai, p. 2.
14. Patai, p. 4.

15. Franklin Delano Roosevelt, *Second Inaugural Address,* in *Bartlett's Familiar Quotations,* Fourteenth Edition (Boston: Little, Brown and Company, 1968), p. 971 b.
16. *Encyclopaedia Britannica,* vol. 4, p. 696.
17. Howard Zinn, *A People's History of the United States* (New York: Harper & Row, 1980), p. 384.
18. *Chronicle of the 20th Century* (Mount Kisco, NY: Chronicle Publications, 1987), p. 426.
19. Zinn, p. 420.

CHAPTER FIVE

1. *Encyclopaedia Britannica,* vol. 5 (Chicago: Encyclopaedia Britannica, 1984), p. 834.
2. Dmitri Volkogonov, *Stalin: Triumph & Tragedy* (New York: Grove Weidenfeld, 1991), p. 206.
3. Robert Conquest, *Stalin and the Kirov Murder* (New York: Oxford University Press, 1989), p. 3.
4. Conquest, p. 26.
5. Conquest, p. 28.
6. Conquest, p. 28.
7. Anonymous, *Kirov, Sergei* (Grolier Multimedia Encyclopedia, 1998).
8. *Encyclopaedia Britannica,* vol. 16, p. 76.
9. Alan Bullock, *Hitler and Stalin: Parallel Lives* (New York: Alfred A. Knopf, 1992), p. 466.
10. Conquest, p. 13.
11. Conquest, p. 42.
12. Bullock, p. 468.
13. Volkogonov, p. 208.
14. Conquest, p. 44.
15. Geoffrey Hosking, *The First Socialist Society: A History of the Soviet Union from Within* (Cambridge, MA: Harvard University Press, 1993), p. 186.
16. Hosking, p. 187.
17. Hosking, p. 188.
18. Robert Conquest, *The Great Terror: Stalin's Purge of the Thirties* (New York: The Macmillan Company, 1968), p. 116.
19. Sir John Lawrence, *A History of Russia* (New York: Meridian, 1993) pp. 282–283.

20. Bullock, p. 488.
21. Bullock, p. 489.
22. Bullock, p. 493.
23. Conquest, *The Great Terror: Stalin's Purge of the Thirties*, pp. 138, 142.
24. Conquest, *Stalin and the Kirov Murder*, p. 97.
25. Bullock, p. 503.

CHAPTER SIX

1. Robert Conquest, *The Great Terror: Stalin's Purge of the Thirties* (New York: The Macmillan Company, 1968), p. 90.
2. Alan Bullock, *Hitler and Stalin: Parallel Lives* (New York: Alfred A. Knopf, 1992), p. 406.
3. Conquest, p. 318.
4. Conquest, pp. 320-321.
5. Conquest, p. 333.
6. Conquest, p. 332.
7. *Encyclopaedia Britannica,* vol. 16 (Chicago: Encyclopaedia Britannica, 1984), p. 75.
8. Bullock, p. 512.
9. Bullock, p. 512.
10. Conquest, p. 336.
11. Conquest, p. 336.
12. Conquest, p. 339.
13. Geoffrey Hosking, *The First Socialist Society: A History of the Soviet Union from Within* (Cambridge, MA: Harvard University Press, 1993), p. 203.
14. Bullock, p. 512.
15. *Encyclopaedia Britannica,* vol. 16, p. 76.

CHAPTER SEVEN

1. William L. Shirer, *The Rise and Fall of the Third Reich: A History of Nazi Germany* (New York: Simon and Schuster, 1960), p. 299.
2. Alan Bullock, *Hitler and Stalin: Parallel Lives* (New York: Alfred A. Knopf, 1992), p. 547.
3. Bullock, p. 399.
4. Bullock, p. 536.
5. Shirer, p. 305.
6. Shirer, p. 307.

7. Bullock, p. 639.
8. Bullock, p. 536.
9. Robert Conquest, *The Great Terror: Stalin's Purge of the Thirties* (New York: The Macmillan Company, 1968), p. 217.
10. Dmitri Volkogonov, *Stalin: Triumph & Tragedy* (New York: Grove Weidenfeld, 1991), p. 348.
11. *Chronicle of the 20th Century* (Mount Kisco, NY: Chronicle Publications, 1987), p. 484.
12. *Chronicle*, p. 485.
13. Shirer, p. 477
14. *Chronicle*, p. 492.
15. Bullock, p. 609.
16. Volkogonov, p. 353.
17. Volkogonov, p. 353.
18. Bullock, p. 609.
19. Volkogonov, p. 353.
20. Volkogonov, p. 354.
21. *Chronicle*, p. 496.
22. *Chronicle*, p. 497.

CHAPTER EIGHT

1. *Chronicle of the 20th Century* (Mount Kisco, NY: Chronicle Publications, 1987), p. 447.
2. *Chronicle*, p. 483.
3. *Chronicle*, p. 487.
4. *Encyclopaedia Britannica*, vol. 5 (Chicago: Encyclopaedia Britannica, 1984), p. 682.
5. *Chronicle*, p. 469.
6. *Encyclopaedia Britannica*, vol. 5, p. 383.
7. *Encyclopaedia Britannica*, vol. 16, p. 73.
8. Dmitri Volkogonov, *Stalin: Triumph & Tragedy* (New York: Grove Weidenfeld, 1991), p. 255.
9. Volkogonov, p. 382.
10. Volkogonov, p. 382.
11. *Chronicle*, p. 513.

12. Alan Bullock, *Hitler and Stalin: Parallel Lives* (New York: Alfred A. Knopf, 1992), pp. 657–658.
13. Bullock, p. 658.
14. Bullock, p. 659.
15. Bullock, p. 660.
16. Bullock, p. 677.
17. *Webster's Universal Unabridged Dictionary: Deluxe Second Edition* (New York: Dorset & Baber, 1979), p. 196.
18. *Encyclopaedia Britannica,* vol. 7 (Chicago: Encyclopaedia Britannica, 1984), p. 961.
19. *Chronicle,* p. 508.
20. *Chronicle,* p. 509.
21. Volkogonov, p. 373.
22. *Encyclopaedia Britannica,* vol. 19, p. 987.
23. Bullock, p. 705.
24. Bullock, pp. 721–722.
25. Lord Acton, *Letter to Bishop Mandell Creighton* in *Bartlett's Familiar Quotations,* Fourteenth Edition (Boston: Little, Brown and Company, 1968), p. 750a.

GLOSSARY

Anti-Comintern Pact—agreement between Germany, Japan, Italy, and others to oppose the Soviet Comintern; secret clauses threatened the Soviet Union itself

blitzkrieg—German for "lightning war"; a swift, sudden, overwhelming attack

Bolsheviks—literally "the majority," they would claim to represent the workers of the world; also an early name for Communists

bourgeoisie—owners of the means of production, and employers of wage laborers

capitalism—private ownership and free trade for profit

collectivization—government takeover of farmlands in order to merge and mechanize them

Comintern (The Third International)—Communist organization formed to promote policies of world revolution

commissar—a head of a department in any of the local or national governments of the USSR

commissariat—a government department headed by a commissar

communism—ownership of all property by the community as a whole

Communist Manifesto—pamphlet in which Karl Marx and Friedrich Engels spelled out the aims of communism

Council of People's Commissars—cabinet made up of the heads of various branches of the Soviet government

cult of personality—identification of the nation and people with the leader

Declaration of the Rights of Peoples—proclamation giving territories of the former tsarist empire the right to secede from Russia and set up independent nations

dekulakization—eliminating the landowning kulaks

Dictatorship of the Proletariat—rule *by* the common people distorted to become rule *of* the common people by Communist despots

fellow travelers—non-Communists involved in causes championed by Communists

Five-Year Plan—specified goals of industrial and agricultural growth

Fourth International—anti-Stalinist organization founded by Trotsky to spread communism

gulag—a primitive prison camp usually set in a remote area

kulaks—wealthy landowners who employed peasants to work their farms

Kuomintang—Chinese military organization, which eventually fought Communists

Leningrad—former Russian capital city; originally St. Petersburg, then Petrograd, now again called St. Petersburg

Marxism—system of Socialist-Communist economics developed by Karl Marx

New Economic Policy (NEP)—Program granting peasants ownership of land and the right to sell

NKVD—Soviet secret police from 1934 to 1946

OGPU—Soviet secret police from 1922 to 1934, when it was reorganized as the NKVD

Operation Barbarossa—June 1941 invasion of the Soviet Union by Nazi Germany

Party Congress—meeting of local Communist party leaders held periodically

party line—Comintern policies for foreign branches of the Communist party and fellow travelers

peasant—farm laborer

Phony War—the 1939–1940 stalemate between German and British-French armies

pogrom—raids in which Jews were robbed, raped, and murdered

Politburo—five-member panel appointed by the Central Committee of the Communist party to make quick decisions in urgent matters

Popular Front—Comintern policy of alignment with non-Communist democratic and left-wing forces

proletariat—workers; those whose only capital is their labor

Provisional Government—body that ruled Russia between abdication of Tsar Nicholas II and the Bolshevik takeover

purge—dispensing with political foes by exile, imprisonment, or execution

Red—Communist

Russian Social Democratic Labour Party—organization that evolved into the Communist party

show trials—Soviet treason hearings carefully orchestrated to prove the guilt of the accused to the press and public

Socialist—one who believes in modified reforms based on Marxist principles

soviet—council of workers

troika—three-person leadership group

Trotskyite—anti-Stalinist who follows Leon Trotsky's teachings

Union of Soviet Socialist Republics (USSR)—collection of nations making up the Soviet Union

urkas—professional criminals who preyed on other prisoners in the gulags

Whites—anti-Communist Russians

Winter War—1939–1940 conflict between the Soviet Union and Finland

zeks—slave laborers in the gulags

FOR MORE INFORMATION

Bullock, Alan. *Hitler and Stalin: Parallel Lives.* New York: Alfred A. Knopf, 1992.

Conquest, Robert. *The Great Terror: Stalin's Purge of the Thirties.* New York: The Macmillan Company, 1968.

Conquest, Robert. *Stalin and the Kirov Murder.* New York: Oxford University Press, 1989.

Crozier, Brian. *The Rise and Fall of the Soviet Empire.* Rocklin, CA: Prima Publishing, 1999.

Gunther, John. *Inside Russia Today.* New York: Harper & Brothers, 1958.

Hosking, Geoffrey. *Russia and the Russians: A History.* Boston: Harvard University Press, 2001.

Lawrence, Sir John. *A History of Russia.* New York: Meridian, 1993.

MacKenzie, David. *A History of Russia and the Soviet Union.* Homewood, IL: Dorset Press, 1977.

Matthews, John R. *The Rise and Fall of the Soviet Union.* San Diego, CA: Lucent Books, 2000.

Miller, William J., Henry L. Roberts, and Marshall D. Shulman. *The Meaning of Communism.* Morristown, NJ: Silver Burdett Company/Time Incorporated, 1963.

Shirer, William L. *The Rise and Fall of the Third Reich: A History of Nazi Germany.* New York: Simon and Schuster, 1960.

Volkogonov, Dmitri. *Autopsy for an Empire: The Seven Leaders Who Built the Soviet Regime.* New York: The Free Press, 1998.

Volkogonov, Dmitri. *Stalin: Triumph & Tragedy.* New York: Grove Weidenfeld, 1988.

INTERNET SITES

The Avalon Project at the Yale Law School: Anti-Comintern Pact
<www.yale.edu/lawweb/avalon/wwii/tri1.htm>

Joseph Stalin Reference Archive: 1879–1953
<www.marxists.org/reference/archive/stalin/>

Modern History Sourcebook: Stalin's Purges, 1935
<www.fordham.edu/halsall/mod/1936purges.html>

The Enemy on Trial: Early Soviet Courts on Stage and Screen by Julie A. Cassiday, Northern Illinois University Press:
<www.niu.edu/univ_press/books/266-4.htm>

This Month in Holocaust History: June 22, 1941: "Operation Barbarossa"
<www.yad-vashem.org.il/molocaust/chronology/June/chronology_1941_june_22.html>

INDEX

Page numbers in *italics* refer to illustrations.